Fishing rule #1:

The least experienced fisherman always catches the biggest fish.

Fishing rule #2:

The worse your line is tangled, the more fish the man beside you will catch.

Fishing rule #3:

Fishing won't make you truthful, but it will make you happy.

The Fishing Fanatic's

GUIDE TO HAPPINESS

Nic van Oudtshoorn

Cartoons by Jackson Graham

MAXIMEDIA

Maximedia is a registered trademark and imprint of
Maximedia Pty Ltd
PO Box 85
Jamberoo NSW 2533
Australia
Website: www.maximedia.com.au
Email: info@maximedia.com.au

ISBN: 978-1-921373-26-8

DISCLAIMER

While every effort has been made to ensure that this book is free from error or omissions, the publisher, author, and their respective employees or agents shall not accept responsibility for injury, loss or damage occasioned by any person acting or refraining from action as a result of material in this book, whether or not such injury, loss or damage is in any way due to any negligent act or omission, breach of duty or default on the part of the publisher, author, or their respective employees or agents.

INTRODUCTION

FISHING IS THE world's greatest — and probably our oldest — sport. From an outback Australian billabong to a hole cut in the Arctic ice, it is pursued by more people in more countries than any other sport. The reason is simple: fishing is a sport with bite ... and once you're hooked, there's no escaping.

For the fishing fanatic, it's also a way of life — the only way of life. And no wonder, for it feeds both body (infrequently) and soul (always). Fishing is also a quest for happiness. Henry David Thoreau explained it this way: "Many men go fishing all their lives without knowing that it is not fish they are after."

Part 1 of *The Fishing Fanatic's Guide to Happiness* brings together the wit and the wisdom of fishing fanatics through the ages who have tried to capture in words a pleasure we all know but find impossible to express.

It is also a survival guide for anglers everywhere, packed with apt advice like this from Mark Twain: "Don't tell fish stories where the people know you; but particularly, don't tell them where they know the fish."

In **Part 2** (starting on page 81) we turn from the wisdom of the sages to the wit of the Web for some of the **funniest fishing tales** around. They're guaranteed to keep you chuckling at your favorite fishing spot.

Spice up this succulent chowder with **wordsearch and maze puzzles**, a **Fishing Dictionary** (page 84), **Monsters of the Deep** (page 105), **Fishinating Facts** (page 125), and great fishing stories by **Jerome K. Jerome** (page 113) and **Zane Grey** (page 135) — and you have a dish that will keep you entertained for hours!

Fishing is much more than fish.
It's the great occasion when we
may return to the fine
simplicity of our forefathers.

— HERBERT HOOVER

Fishing is a delusion
entirely surrounded by
liars in old clothes.

— DON MARQUIS

Fishes live in the sea, as men do
a-land; the great ones
eat up the little ones.

— WILLIAM SHAKESPEARE

If people concentrated on the
really important
things in life, there'd be a
shortage of fishing poles.

— DOUG LARSON

"I THINK IT'S MY NEW ANTIPERSPIRANT !!"

We eat fish and fish eat us.

— Dana Scully

Those who won't get their feet wet don't catch fish.

— Chinese proverb

A man may fish with the worm that hath eat of a king, And eat of the fish that hath fed of that worm.

— William Shakespeare

You won't find one fish in a million that has enough sense to come in when it rains.

— Robert Benchley

If fishing is a religion, fly-fishing is high church.

—Tom Brokaw

"THE FISH COURSE IS OFF...
NO ONE CAUGHT ANY!"

Chance is always powerful.
Let your hook be always cast;
in the pool where you least
expect it, there will be a fish.

— Ovid

Govern a family as you would
cook a small fish — very gently.

— Chinese proverb

If you tell Congress everything
about the world situation,
they get hysterical. If you tell
them nothing, they go fishing.

— Harry S. Truman

The books all say that barracuda
rarely eat people, but very few
barracuda can read.

— Dave Barry

"I'M USING A REAL FLY . . . ."

Call intuition cosmic fishing.
You feel a nibble, then you've
got to hook the fish.

— BUCKMINSTER FULLER

Time is but the stream I go
a-fishin' in. I drink at it, but while
I drink I see the sandy bottom
and detect how shallow it is.
Its thin current slides
away, but eternity remains.

— HENRY DAVID THOREAU

The man who goes fishing
gets something more
than the fishes he catches.

— MARY ASTOR

If you think fly-fishermen are
unusual, talk to a mushroom-hunter.

— JOHN GIERACH

" POACHERS ?"

Ten years from now I plan to be
sitting here, looking out
over my land. I hope I'll be
writing books, but if not, I'll be
on my pond fishing with my kids.
I feel like the luckiest guy
I know.

— JOHN GRISHAM

It is admirable for a man to take
his son fishing, but there is a
special place in heaven
for the father who takes his
daughter shopping.

— JOHN SINOR

Last year I went fishing with
Salvador Dali.
He was using a dotted line.
He caught every other fish.

— STEVEN WRIGHT

"HOW DID HE DO THAT ? — I'VE
BEEN AFTER THAT FISH FOR THE
LAST TWELVE MONTHS !"

Fishing gives you a sense of
where you fit in the scheme
of things — your place in the
universe ... I mean, here I am,
one small guy with a fishing pole
on this vast beach and out there
in the blue expanse of ocean are
these hundreds of millions of fish
... laughing at me.

— A.J.P Taylor

Man can learn a lot from fishing
— when the fish are biting no
problem in the world is big
enough to be remembered.

— O. A. Battista

I love fishing. It's like
transcendental meditation
with a punch line.

— Billy Connolly

To my purist trout-fishing friends, bass are lowly green fish and brown fish. To me, bass are bent rods and aching arms. To my ex-wife, bass are the bewilderment of addiction.

— JIM SLINSKY

The two best times to fish are when it's rainin' and when it ain't.

— PATRICK F. MCMANUS

A trout is a moment of beauty known only to those who seek it.

— ARNOLD GRINGRICH

I don't know exactly what fly fishing teaches us, but I think it's something we need to know.

— JOHN GIERACH

"THE DOWNSIDE TO THIS IS, KNOWING WE'RE NEVER GOING TO GET A BITE!"

The fishing was good — it's the catching that was poor.

— A.K. BEST

The fisherman has a harmless, preoccupied look; he is a kind of vagrant, that nothing fears. He blends himself with the trees and the shadows. All his approaches are gentle and indirect. He times himself to the meandering, soliloquising stream; he addresses himself to it as a lover to his mistress; he woos it and stays with it till he knows its hidden secrets.

— JOHN BURROUGHS

A bad day of fishing is better than a good day at work.

— ANON.

" TWO ! IS THAT ALL ... AND YOU
CALL YOURSELVES FISHERMAN ".

There is a fine line between
fishing and just standing
on the shore like an idiot.

— STEVEN WRIGHT

The weather for catching fish
is that weather, and no
other, in which fish are caught.

— W.H. BLAKE

Angling may be said to be so
like mathematics that
it can never be fully learnt.

— IZAAK WALTON

To him, all good things — trout as
well as eternal salvation — come
by grace and grace comes by art
and art does not come easy.

— NORMAN MACLEAN

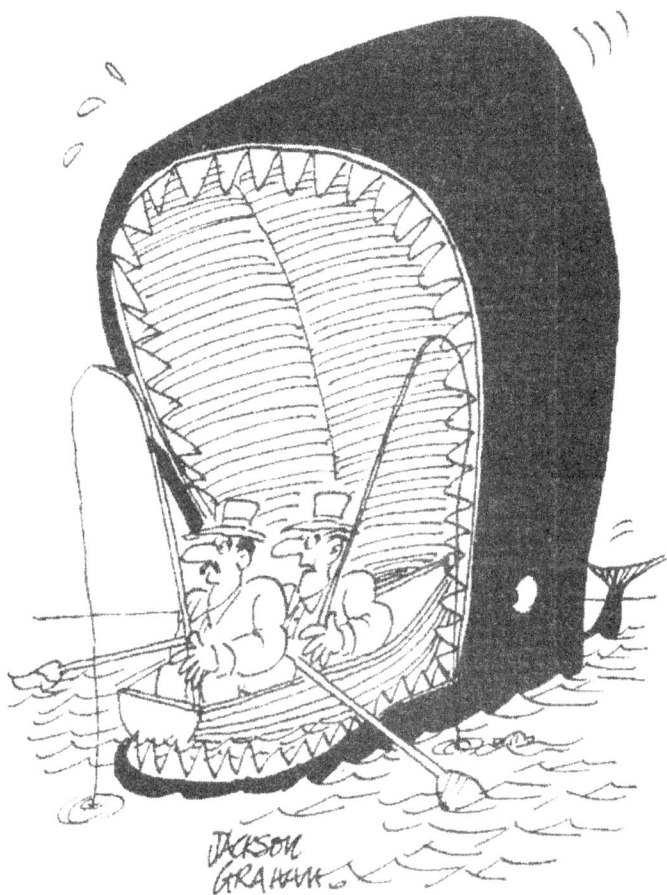

"IT'S GETTING DARK AND WE HAVEN'T HAD A BITE ALL DAY!"

To me heaven would be a big
bullring with me holding two
barrera seats and a trout stream
outside that no one else was
allowed to fish in and two lovely
houses in the town;
one where I would have my wife
and children and be monogamous
and love them truly and well and
the other where I would have
my nine beautiful mistresses on
nine different floors.

— ERNEST HEMINGWAY

The perch swallows the
grub-worm, the pickerel swallows
the perch, and the fisherman
swallows the pickerel;
and so on the chinks in the scale
of being are filled.

— HENRY DAVID THOREAU

"YOU'LL HAVE TO THROW HER BACK
— YOU'RE A VEGETARIAN!"

We were 'catching fish' rather
than 'getting one now and then'.
If you are not a fisherman,
I can't begin to explain the
importance of that distinction.

— JOHN GIERACH

No human being, however
great, or powerful,
was ever so free as a fish.

— JOHN RUSKIN

We may say of angling, as
Dr Boteler said of strawberries,
'Doubtless God could have made
a better berry, but doubtless God
never did'; and so, if I might be
judge, God never did make a more
calm, quiet, innocent recreation
than angling.

— IZAAK WALTON

"WHY DO YOU ALWAYS GIVE ME THE IMPRESSION YOU'RE MIXING PLEASURE WITH BUSINESS?"

When I sit by the river, my mind is totally concentrated on fishing and nothing else. I have a good feel for the give and pull of the line so the fish are not even aware when the hook and bait enter the water.
To them, the bait is no different from a grain of sand or a bubble, and they swallow it without suspecting.
This is the principle of using the soft to win over the strong and the light to hold the heavy.
My lord, if you can rule your country this way, then everything in the world will be at your fingertips.
Isn't that more effective than using force?

— TAOIST HERMIT LIEH TZU AROUND 400BCE

"I WANT SOME MICE FOR BAIT — I'M GOING AFTER CAT FISH".

Somebody just back of you
while you are fishing is as bad
as someone looking over your
shoulder while you write
a letter to your girl.

— ERNEST HEMINGWAY

Unless one can enjoy himself
fishing with the fly, even when his
efforts are unrewarded, he
loses much real pleasure.
More than half the intense
enjoyment of fly-fishing is
derived from the beautiful
surroundings, the satisfaction felt
from being in the open air, the
new lease of life secured thereby,
and the many, many pleasant
recollections of all
one has seen, heard and done.

— CHARLES F. ORVIS

"DO YOU THINK THEY KNOW
SOMETHING WE DON'T KNOW?!!"

In a way, fishing is like the best photography: it doesn't so much copy something as it freezes an instant in time.

— John Gierach

All you need to be a fisherman is patience and a worm.

— Herb Shriner

Still he fishes that catches one.

—Thomas Fuller

Fishing seems to be the favourite form of loafing.

— Edgar Watson Howe

I am not against golf, since it keeps armies of the unworthy from discovering trout.

— Paul O'Neil

"I SNAPPED ALL MY FISHING TACKLE FOR HIM."

The trout fly does not resemble
any known species of insect.
It is a 'conventionalised' creation,
as we say of ornamentation.
The theory is that, fly-fishing
being a high art, the fly
must not be a tame imitation
of nature, but an artistic
suggestion of it.
It requires an artist to
construct one; and not every
bungler can take a bit of red
flannel, a peacock's feather,
a flash of tinsel thread,
a cock's plume, a section
of hen's wing, and fabricate
a tiny object that will not
look like any fly, but will
still suggest the universal
conventional fly.

— CHARLES DUDLEY WARNER

"WOW! MY FIRST CATCH. A SIZE TEN!"

Fishing is a sport invented by insects and you are the bait.

— Anon.

Fly-fishing is like sex: everyone thinks there is more than there is, and that everyone is getting more than their share.

— Henry Kanemoto

I'm glad when the fish
I catch get away.
There isn't room in
the boat for both of us.

— Anon.

See how he throws his
baited lines about,
And plays his men as
anglers play their trout.

— O. W. Holmes

"...AND THE ANNUAL MEMBERSHIP FEE ENTITLES YOU TO TWO FREE STRESS COUNSELLING SESSIONS WHEN YOU HAVEN'T CAUGHT ANYTHING".

It is well known that no person
who regards his reputation
will ever kill a trout with
anything but a fly.
It requires some training
on the part of the trout
to take to this method.
The uncultivated, unsophisticated
trout in unfrequented waters
prefers the bait; and the
rural people, whose sole
object in going a-fishing
appears to be to catch fish,
indulge them in their
primitive taste for the worm.
No sportsman however, will use
anything but the fly,
except when he happens
to be alone.

— CHARLES DUDLEY WARNER

"THAT WON'T CATCH ON. CLUBBING THEM'S LOTS MORE FUN."

Canst thou draw out
leviathan with a hook?

— OLD TESTAMENT; JOB, XLI, 1.

The man that weds
for greedy wealth,
He goes a fishing fair,
But oftentimes he gets a frog,
Or very little share.

— ANON.

They may the better fish in the
water when it is troubled.

— RICHARD GRAFTON

Simon Peter saith unto them,
I go a fishing.
They say unto him:
We also go with thee.

— NEW TESTAMENT: JOHN, XXI,3.

"HE'S NOT STUPID. HE SENSES
YOU'RE A FISHING MANIAC".

If you want happiness
for an hour
— take a nap.
If you want happiness for a day
— go fishing.
If you want happiness
for a month
— get married.
If you want happiness for a year
— inherit a fortune.
If you want happiness
for a lifetime
— help someone else.

— CHINESE PROVERB

The charm of fishing is that it is
the pursuit of what is elusive, but
attainable, a perpetual series of
occasions for hope.

— JOHN BUCHAN, LORD TWEEDSMUIR

"THERE GOES 18 STONE OF MUSCLE TO FIGHT A 2½ lb TROUT TO THE DEATH!"

Can the fish love the fisherman?

(PISCATOREM PISCIS AMARE POTEST?)

— MARTIAL, EPIGRAMS

I guess you have to remember that those who don't fish often see those of us who do as harmlessly strange and sort of amusing. When you think about it, that might be a fair assessment.

— JOHN GIERACH

Angling: incessant expectation ... and perpetual disappointment.

— ANON.

Never a fisherman
need there be,
If fishes could hear
as well as see.

— ANON.

"I TAKE IT THIS IS THE LAST OF THE SALMON I CAUGHT!"!"

When the wind is in the east,
Then the fishes bite the least;
When the wind is in the west,
Then the fishes bite the best;
When the wind is in the north,
Then the fishes do come forth;
When the wind is in the south,
It blows the bait in the fish's mouth.

— ANON.

A fishing-rod is a stick with a
hook at one end
and a fool at the other.

— SAMUEL JOHNSON

'Tis an affair of luck.

— HENRY VAN DYKE, FISHERMAN'S LUCK

There's none of our employments
With fishing can compare.

— ANON.

"THAT'S THE BEST CATCH HE'S HAD ALL YEAR!"

Of all the world's enjoyments
that ever valued were,
Fishing is an art worthy the
knowledge and patience
of a wise man.

— ANON.

There is certainly something in
fishing that tends to produce
a gentleness of spirit, a pure
serenity of mind.

— WASHINGTON IRVING

The fun of fishing
is catching 'em,
not killing 'em.

— NORMAN SCHWARZKOPF

Listen to the sound of the river
and you will get a trout.

— IRISH PROVERB

"YOU'VE GONE TO YOUR SPECIAL PLACE AGAIN, HAVEN'T YOU..?"

Fly-fishing is the most fun you can have standing up.

— ARNOLD GINDRICH

O, sir, doubt not that Angling is an art; is it not an art to deceive a trout with an artificial fly?

— IZAAK WALTON

Here comes the trout that must be caught with tickling.

— WILLIAM SHAKESPEARE, *TWELTH NIGHT*

If fishing is interfering with your business, give up your business.

— ALFRED W. MILLER

My wife said to me that if I go fishing once more she will leave me. God, I will miss her!

— ANON.

"YOU'RE SUFFERING FROM 'BORING FISHERMAN'S SYNDROME'. TAKE UP GOLF FOR A WHILE".

In my family, there was no clear division between religion and fly-fishing.

— Norman Maclean

The difference between fly-fishers and worm dunkers is the quality of their excuses.

— Anon.

You will find angling to be like the virtue of humility, which has a calmness of spirit and a world of other blessings attending upon it.

— Anon.

Some go to church and think about fishing, others go fishing and think about God.

— Tony Blake

"SO, THIS IS YOUR FIRST BIG GAME FISH FISHING TRIP?"

Rivers and the inhabitants of the watery elements are made for wise men to contemplate.

— Izaak Walton

There are only two occasions when Americans respect privacy, especially in presidents. Those are prayer and fishing.

— Herbert Hoover

It is to be observed that 'angling' is the name given to fishing by people who can't fish.

— Stephen B. Leacock

Calling fly-fishing a hobby is like calling brain surgery a job.

— Paul Schullery

"CALL AT THE FISHSHOP ON YOUR WAY HOME AND GET SOME FISH FOR TEA"

Enjoy thy stream, oh harmless fish,
And when an angler for his dish,
Through gluttony's vile sin,
Attempts – a wretch
– to pull thee out
God give thee strength,
oh, gentle trout,
To pull the rascal in.

— PETER PINDAR, *TESTAMENT OF A FISHERMAN*

He fishes well who
uses a golden hook.

— LATIN PROVERB

As no man is born an artist,
so no man is born an angler.

— ANON.

A trout is a fish known
mainly by hearsay.

H.T. PHILLIPS

"FOR GOD SAKE, PUT SOME CLOTHES ON — YOU'LL FRIGHTEN THE FISH!"

Doubt not but angling
will prove to be
so pleasant
that it will prove to be,
like virtue,
a reward to itself.

— ANON.

Fish should smell
like the tide.
Once they smell
like fish,
it's too late.

— OSCAR GIZELT

If you don't go fishing because
you think it might rain,
you will never go fishing.
This applies to more
than fishing.

— GARY SOW

"HE CATCHES ALL KINDS OF THINGS WHEN HE'S FISHING. COLDS...FLU...LUMBAGO ... RHEUMATISM...."

There are two kinds
of fishermen.
Those who fish
for sport
and those who
catch something.

— ANON.

I fished a lot, dove a lot,
boated a lot — and made
Johnny Walker Red
about a quarter
of a million dollars richer.

— DENNIS DIAZ

Technology is like a fish.
The longer it stays
on the shelf,
the less desirable
it becomes.

— ANDREW HELLER

"I DON'T MIND YOUR CLUB'S GUARD OF HONOUR — BUT DID THEY HAVE TO BRING THE FISH ?!!"

The only kind of seafood
I trust is the fish stick,
a totally featureless
fish that doesn't
have eyeballs or fins.

— DAVE BARRY

If you are lucky, sooner
or later there will be a
swirl or a double swirl
where the trout strikes and
misses and strikes again, and
then the old deathless thrill of
the plunge of the rod
and the irregular plunging,
circling, cutting up stream and
shooting into the air
fight the big trout puts up,
no matter what country
he may be in.

— ERNEST HEMINGWAY

"DAMNED FLYING-FISH POACHERS!"

It is not a fish until
it is on the bank.

— IRISH PROVERB

The attraction of angling for all
ages of man, from the cradle to
the grave, lies in its uncertainty.

— HENRY VAN DYKE

The curious thing about fishing is
that you never want to go home.
If you catch anything,
you can't stop.
If you don't catch anything,
you hate to leave
in case something might bite.

— GLADYS TABER

Fish are good. You know where
you stand with fish.

— FALCON STARTREDDER

"THAT'S 'MAD MICK'. HE TRIED
TICKLING PIRANHA !"

Probably that was the
moment that all the
bickering and talk back of
husbands and wives
originated; when Adam
called to Eve to come and
look at his first fish
while it was still silver
and vivid in its living colours;
and Eve answered
that she was busy.

— CHRISTOPHER MORLEY

There is a peculiar pleasure in
catching a trout in a place
where nobody thinks of
looking for them,
and at an hour when
everybody believes they
cannot be caught.

— HENRY VAN DYKE

"HE DIDN'T PUT UP
MUCH OF A FIGHT".

Our idea of fishing is to
put all the exertion
up to the fish.
If they are ambitious
we will catch them.
If they are not,
let them go about
their business.

— DON MARQUIS

A beautiful stream to one man
is to another just so much water
in which he may possibly
catch so many fish.

— ARTHUR BRISBANE

There is no use in your walking
five miles to fish when you
can depend on being just as
unsuccessful near home.

— MARK TWAIN

"BELIEVE ME. THIS IS THE BEST WAY TO CATCH THEM. THEY CAN'T RESIST A TARGET ..."

If there is to be adequate
chivalry in the pastime
no man should be allowed a rod
and line until he has
first signed an agreement that
every time he fails to pull a
hooked fish out of the water
he himself will accept
and signal defeat
by jumping into the lake.
The man gets the fish
or the fish gets the man.
I can see no other fair way.

— HEYWOOD BROUN

All men are mad who devote
themselves to the pursuit of
power when they could be
fishing, painting pictures,
or simply sitting in the sun.

— ANON.

" COVER UP YOUR BITS, MATE —
THERE ARE SOME VERY AGGRESIVE
FISH IN THE LAKE !"

Bragging may not bring
happiness, but no man having
caught a large fish
goes home through an alley.

— ANON.

The water in that river is so
polluted that if you catch a
bream, he thanks you.

— ED WALKER

I think fish are nice,
but then I think that
rain is wet, so
who am I to judge?

— DOUGLAS ADAMS

I've spent most of
my life fishing.
The rest of it I wasted.

— DICK SAUNDERS

"WELL, I CAN'T FIND ANYTHING
IN THE RULES ABOUT IT!"

Some people are under the impression that all that is required to make a good fisherman is the ability to tell lies easily and without blushing; but this is a mistake. Mere bald fabrication is useless; the greenest novice can manage that. It is in the circumstantial detail, the embellishing touches of probability, the general air of scrupulous – almost of pedantic – veracity, that the experienced angler is seen.

— JEROME K. JEROME

For a man to admit a distaste for fishing would be like denouncing mother-love or hating moonlight.

— JOHN STEINBECK

"HERE COME THE
STURGEON FISHERMEN."

How much fishing tackle
can a man accumulate
before his wife
throws him out ?
I don't know the answer
— but I believe
I'm nearly there.

— DICK SAUNDERS

A wife and a steady job
have ruined many a good
fisherman.

— ED WALKER

Earth's surface is three quarters
water and one quarter land.
Clearly God intended man to
spend triple the time
fishing than doing gardening.

— ANON.

"I THINK WE'VE GOT HIM
WORRIED, LADS!"

Give a man a fish, and you
feed him for a day.
Teach him how to fish and
you feed him for a lifetime.

— Lao Tzu

Give a man a fish and he will live
for a day. Teach a man how
to fish and he will ... every day.

— Anon.

Give a man a fish, and you feed
him for a day. Teach a man to fish
and he will bore you stupid.

— Lorrie B. Poners

If you give a man a fish he will
eat for a day. If you teach a man
to fish he will drink beer, tell lies
and wear a stupid hat.

— Anon.

"SOME OF THESE HYBRID FISH ARE GETTING A BIT BLASÉ...."

Give a man a fish
and he'll fish for a day.
But if you train a man to fish,
he'll fish for a lifetime.

— DAN QUALE

Catch a man a fish
and you can sell it to him.
Teach a man to fish
and you'll ruin a wonderful
business opportunity.

—KARL MARX

Give a man a fish
and you'll feed him
for a day.
Teach him how to fish
and you can get rid of him
for the entire weekend.

— ZENNA SCHAFFER

FUNNY FISH TAILS

SEAMUS was an Irish priest who loved to fly-fish. But every Saturday the weather was awful, and on Sundays he had to work.

Finally, one beautiful Sunday, Seamus just had to go fishing. So he called a fellow priest, Father Jack, and croaked that he had lost his voice and was stuck in bed with the flu. Feeling sorry for him, Jack kindly offered to give the sermon that week. No sooner was the deed done, than Seamus packed up his gear and secretly drove fifty miles to a river.

But an angel up in heaven was keeping watch and saw what the priest was doing. He told God, who agreed Seamus should learn his lesson.

Seamus cast his line and immediately a huge fish gulped down the fly. For the next hour the priest fought the mighty monster. Finally, panting with exertion, he pulled the huge salmon out of the river.

Confused, the angel asked God, "Why did you let him catch that huge fish? I thought that you were going to teach him a lesson."

God replied with a mischievous smile, "That's

what I just did. Who do you think he's going to tell?"

A FISHERMAN'S wife is sitting on the bank of a river, bored to tears. Along comes a fisheries inspector, who asks to speak to her husband .

Pointing to the reeds she replies: "Go over there and look for the pole with a worm on both ends."

WHAT do you call a fly-fisherman who can't get enough?

A 'nympho'!

WHILE on holiday in Australia, an American business man spent a few days at a small fishing town. One morning, while standing at the pier, a small boat with just one fisherman docked. Inside the small boat were ten large yellow-fin tuna.

"Your fish sure look fine," complimented the American. "Have you been out long?"

"No mate," said the Australian fisherman. "It's

good fishing around here."

"So why don't you stay out longer and catch more fish?" asked the American.

The Australian replied that he caught enough to make a living. With the rest of his time he slept late, fished a little, played with the kids, and had a few beers.

The American scoffed, "I am a Harvard MBA and could help you. You should spend more time fishing. With the money you earn you could buy a bigger boat. Soon you could buy more boats, and eventually you'd have a fleet of fishing boats. Finally, you could open a cannery, and sell your fish overseas. Then you could leave this little town to run your business in New York or London."

The Australian considered all this for a minute. "So how long will this all take?" he asked.

"Probably about 20 years," answered the American. "And then when the time is right, you can sell your company to the highest bidder for millions! You'd be rich."

"But what then?" asked the Australian.

The American said, 'Then you would retire. Move to a small town near the sea, sleep late, fish a little, play with the kids, and have a few beers with your friends."

"Mate," said the Australian, smiling. "What do you think I'm doing now?"

Fishing dictionary

Angler: An obsessed individual who owns a derelict house, but a clean, shiny boat.

Catch and release: What a true conservationist does usually just before a fishing inspector comes to check his limit.

Hook: (1) A curved piece of metal used to catch fish. (2) A clever advertisement that encourages a fisherman to spend hundreds of dollars on a new rod and reel. (3) A punch given by his wife to a fisherman who has spent too much money on new fishing gear.

Line: Something you tell your friends when they ask how many fish you caught last weekend.

Live bait: The biggest fish you'll hold all day.

Quiet water: The lake after you stop cursing your bad luck and fall asleep at the reel.

Reel: A weighted object that causes a rod to sink quickly when dropped overboard.

Rod: A length of painted fiberglass designed to keep a fisherman from getting close to a fish.

Sinker: What your friends call your boat.

School: A place where fish learn to take the bait from your hook without getting caught on it.

Tackle: What a fisherman's wife does to him when he reaches for his credit card to pay for a new rod and reel.

Tackle box: A box containing a large assortment of sharp objects, all lying so that they can't be picked up without slitting your finger.

Thumb: A temporary hook holder.

Wading: The most common means by which a dry fly fisherman is transformed into a wet fly-fisherman.

THE annual Hicksville fishing tournament was under way, when a funeral procession drove by the lake. All the competitors kept on fishing ... except for Jim, who put his fishing pole down, stood up and removed his hat until the procession had passed.

Another competitor was so impressed by Jim's actions that he went over to talk to him. "I saw how considerate you were toward that funeral procession," he said. "I wish I'd been as thoughtful."

Jim replied, "I reckon it's the least I could do.

After all, we were married for nearly 30 years."

Two fishermen were out on the lake having a great day, pulling in fish after fish, until the boat was full.

When it was time to leave, Fred says, "The fishing here is great! I really hope we can find this spot next time."

"No problem," says John, "I can fix that!" He pulls out a piece of chalk, and draws a big "X" on the side of the boat. "Now, we'll know where this place is next time."

Halfway back to shore, Fred says, "Wait a minute, John! What if we don't get the same boat?"

"How was the fishing today, Mick?" asks his friend, Albie, one Saturday evening.

"Not great," says Mick with a shrug. "I only got fifty bites ... one small fish and forty nine mosquitoes."

"WAITER, waiter! There is a fly in my soup!"

The waiter comes over and picks the fly out of the soup, then carefully looks it over.

He calmly says to the diner, "Sir, your fly is a size 14 iron blue dun. May I recommend it with the poached rainbow trout?"

A SMALL boy says to his father: "Hey Dad, that's a really good fish you caught. Can I use it for bait?"

DAVE has been fishing all night and all day, but hasn't caught a thing. On his way home he goes into the fish shop, where he buys six bream.

"Would you like me to wrap them, sir?" asks the sales assistant.

"No thanks," replies Dave. "But I need to ask a favor.

"Could you throw them to me gently, one by one?"

The sales assistant looks at him strangely. "Yes, sir, I can — but why?"

"Well," explains Dave. "If I catch those fish, I can honestly say when I get home that I caught six bream."

Mystery maze #1

Start at top, end at bottom. Answer on Page 161.

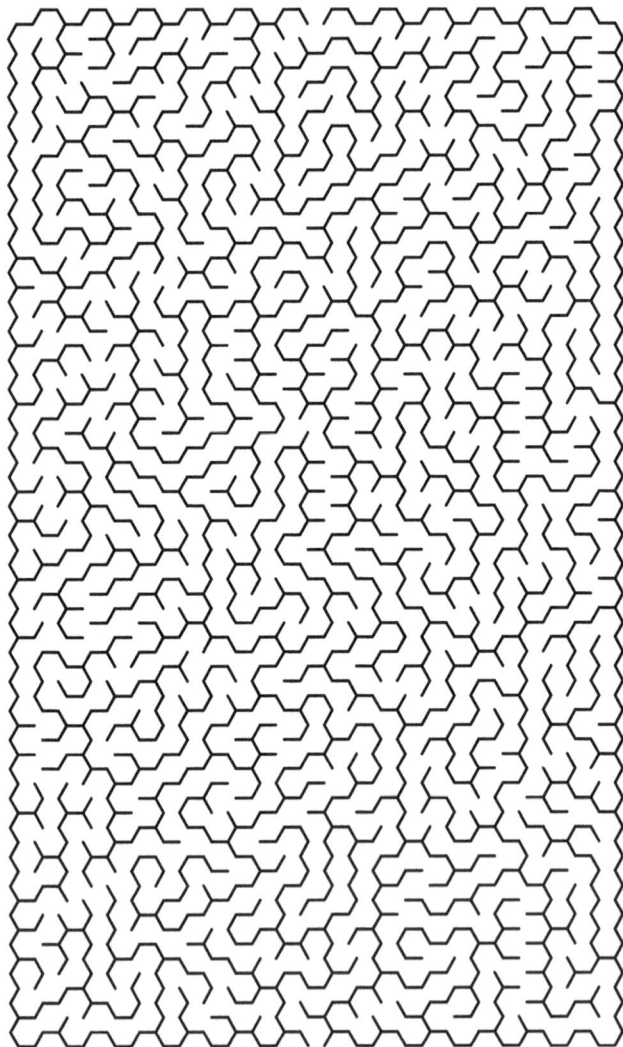

"Okay," said the sales assistant, "but I suggest you take the snapper."

"But why?"

"Because your wife came in earlier today, and said that if you came by, I should tell you to take snapper. She wants that for dinner tonight."

A COUNTRY doctor was famous in the area for always catching large fish.

One day he was on a fishing trip, when he got a mobile phone call that a woman at a nearby farm was giving birth.

He rushed to her aid and delivered a healthy baby girl. The farmer had nothing to weigh the baby with, so the doctor used his fishing scale.

The baby weighed 22 pounds 10 ounces!

Two Canadian anglers are out ice fishing and not even getting a nibble. They look over and see a young boy with a pile of fish next to him. So they wander over to say hello.

As they approach, they notice the young boy catching yet another.

"I can't figure out what he's doing that we're not," says one man to the other.

"Let's ask. Hey, what are you using for bait?"

"Wmmmms" replies the boy.

"Worms?" they ask.

"Yes."

"Hum, that's strange, that's what we're using and we're not even getting a nibble. What's your secret?"

The boy looks at them and mumbles, "U mt kp tm wm".

"What?" reply the men.

The boy spits out a mess of worms and says, "I said, you got to keep them warm."

WALKING by the river one day, Bob notices a one-armed fisherman casting and catching fish. As he watches, the fisherman hooks a huge fish.

The one-armed man sticks his rod in his mouth as he battles the monster. Bob hurries down to the man, quickly grabs his net, and tries to scoop the gigantic fish out of the river. But the huge fish breaks the line and swims away!

"Wow," says Bob. "Did you see how big that fish was?"

"Yes," says the fisherman. He holds up his one arm as he solemnly answers, "It was about this big."

Two fishermen are talking over a beer at the pub.

Jim says to the Peter, "You know, mate, I am NEVER going to take my wife fishing with me ever again!"

"That bad, huh?" asks Peter.

"She did everything wrong!" exclaims Jim. "She talked too much, made the boat rock constantly, tried to stand up in the boat, baited the hook wrong, used the wrong lures and, worst of all, she caught more fish than me!"

A COUPLE on a fishing holiday in Tasmania had a fight when they were fishing a mountain lake.

Jane stormed back to the hotel, but when Michael hadn't returned several hours later she became worried.

She alerted the local amateur mountain-rescue team to ask for help.

While Jane waited in the hotel, Michael strolled back in the evening light after a great day's fishing.

As he dumped his fishing gear in his car he saw the mountaineers preparing to leave.

On asking what the fuss was about, he was told that someone was lost in the mountains.

"I'm all geared-up for the hills," he replied. "I'll give you a hand!" And spent the night searching for himself!

WANTED

WOMAN who can cook, clean, wash and make sweet love. Must have own boat. If interested, send a photo of the boat to...

WHILE fishing in a river, an American, a New Zealander and an Australian were being eaten alive by midges.

"You may think that this is bad," said the Australian, "but back home these insects are so dense that they completely obscure your car windscreen."

Not to be outdone, the Kiwi replies, "Well, in New Zealand, the mosquitoes are so big that our low-flying fighter aircraft have grilles over their air-intakes to prevent them from being clogged by the insects."

Determined to keep up his national pride, the American thought for a few seconds, then said, "Yeah, but in the States the mosquitoes are so big that they have grilles over their air intakes to prevent them from being clogged by low-flying aircraft!"

ON SUNDAY evening, Reverend Smythe met one of his parishioners returning from a day's fishing. The man hadn't been to church for months, so the Reverend stopped him for a chat.

"Ah Jim," he began in his best preaching tone, "I can see from your catch that you are a fine fisherman, but it is better to be a fisher of men, as l am."

Jim looked the Reverend up and down with a smile. "Well, mate, I was passing your church this morning and looked in the window, but you hadn't caught many. Maybe you should change your bait!"

WHAT'S the difference between a hunter and a fisherman?

A hunter lies in wait. A fisherman waits and lies.

EARLY one Saturday morning, Harry took his young son, Andy, fishing. Later that day Andy rushed into the house, crying.

"What happened, darling?" asked his mother, concerned.

"Daddy and I were fishing, and he hooked a giant fish. It was huge.

"Then, while he was reeling it in, the line broke and the fish got away."

"Now come on, Andy," his mother said, "that's not so bad. A big boy like you shouldn't be crying about an accident like that. You should have just laughed it off."

"But that's just what I did, Mum."

Two mates decide to go on a fishing trip. They rent all the equipment they need: the reels, the rods, the wading suits, the rowboat, the car, and even a cabin near a lake. All this costs a fortune.

The first day they go fishing, they don't catch a thing. The second day is the same, and so is the third.

Finally, on the last day of their holiday, one of the men catches a tiny little trout.

As they're driving home, one man says to the

other: "Do you realize that this one stupid fish we caught cost us one thousand dollars?"

"Wow!" says his friend in amazement. "Then it's a good thing we didn't catch any more!"

A PASTOR, a priest and a rabbi were out for a day of fishing.

Their boat had just pulled away from the jetty, when the rabbi realized he'd forgotten to bring his thermos.

The priest, who was driving the boat, offered to turn around.

"Never mind," said the rabbi. "Just wait here — I won't be long!"

So out he jumped, and ran lightly across the water to shore where he grabbed his thermos before coming back the same way.

The pastor watched in amazement. But, not to be outdone, he said loudly "Well, I forgot my sandwiches." Before the priest could offer to turn the boat around the pastor jumped out — and sank to the bottom of the lake!

"Really!" said the priest angrily to the rabbi. "I know he can be a pain, but you should have shown him where the rocks were."

Watery words

Can you find the hidden words in this puzzle?
Level = Easy. Words can go ➔ ⬇

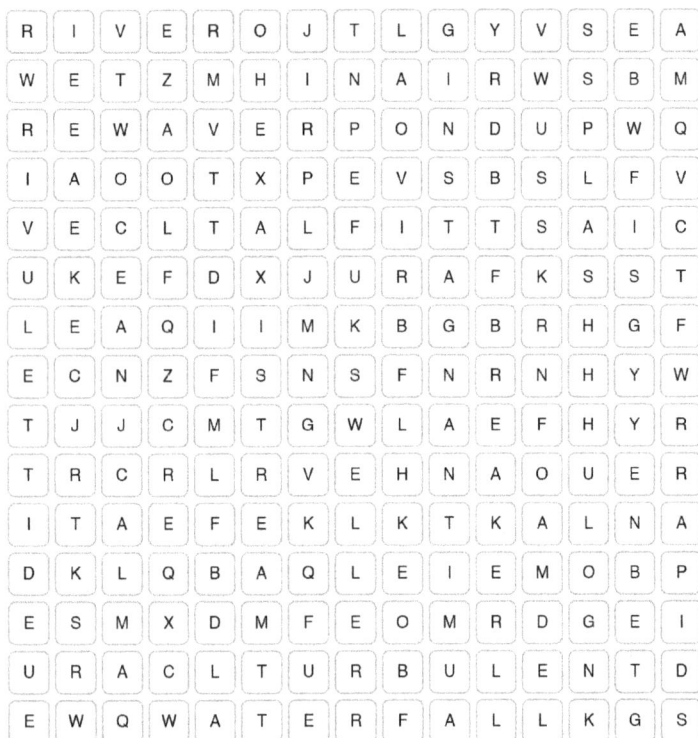

R	I	V	E	R	O	J	T	L	G	Y	V	S	E	A
W	E	T	Z	M	H	I	N	A	I	R	W	S	B	M
R	E	W	A	V	E	R	P	O	N	D	U	P	W	Q
I	A	O	O	T	X	P	E	V	S	B	S	L	F	V
V	E	C	L	T	A	L	F	I	T	T	S	A	I	C
U	K	E	F	D	X	J	U	R	A	F	K	S	S	T
L	E	A	Q	I	I	M	K	B	G	B	R	H	G	F
E	C	N	Z	F	S	N	S	F	N	R	N	H	Y	W
T	J	J	C	M	T	G	W	L	A	E	F	H	Y	R
T	R	C	R	L	R	V	E	H	N	A	O	U	E	R
I	T	A	E	F	E	K	L	K	T	K	A	L	N	A
D	K	L	Q	B	A	Q	L	E	I	E	M	O	B	P
E	S	M	X	D	M	F	E	O	M	R	D	G	E	I
U	R	A	C	L	T	U	R	B	U	L	E	N	T	D
E	W	Q	W	A	T	E	R	F	A	L	L	K	G	S

RIVER	RAPIDS	STAGNANT
CALM	SPLASH	SEA
SWELL	STREAM	POND
TIDE	OCEAN	WAVE
TURBULENT	FOAM	
BREAKER	WATERFALL	
WET	RIVULET	Answer Page 159.

A fisherman's philosophy

A SURE way to get a bite on a slow day is:

1. Talk about changing spots.

2. Prepare another rod while one is out.

3. Lay your rod down unsecured.

4. Start to pull the boat anchor.

5. Use the worst fly you own.

6. Open your first beer.

7. Open your last beer.

8. Put your landing net out of reach.

9. Start reeling in your lines at going home time.

10. Hand your fishing rod to your wife or girlfriend to hold for a while.

Most lures fall into one of these two categories:

- The lures that a fisherman swears always work, and that he will generously lend to you.

- The lures he carefully hides away - because they really work!

A FISHERMAN's wife gave birth to healthy twin boys. When the babies were laid beside each other, they always looked in opposite directions. So their proud parents decided to call them "Forward" and "Away".

On their 18th birthday, the fisherman took his sons fishing, but they didn't return.

The next day, the fisherman sadly came home, alone. "What happened?" asked his wife in tears. "Where are the boys?"

The fisherman shook his head sorrowfully. "While we were fishing, Forward hooked an enormous fish. He fought it for hours, but then suddenly the fish pulled Forward into the water. He disappeared under the crashing waves. We'll never see him again."

"That's just awful!" wept his wife.

"It was awful all right," said the fisherman. "But you should have seen the one that got Away."

A MAN was coming back from fishing at a lake when a fisheries inspector stopped him.

"Excuse me, but do you have a license to catch those fish?" he asked the fisherman.

"Well, no", the man replied. "But don't worry, I didn't catch these. They're my pet fish."

"Pet fish?" the inspector queried.

"That's right. Every night I take them down to the lake and let them swim around for a while. When I whistle they jump back into their buckets, and I take them home to their tank."

"No way! Fish can't do that!"

The man looked at the inspector for a moment, then said, "It's true. Here, I'll show you."

"I've got to see this," said the inspector, and followed the man back to the lake.

Gently the man poured the fish in to the lake, then stood and waited.

After a few minutes, the inspector turned to the man and said: "Well?"

"Well what?" the man responded.

"Well, when are you going to whistle and call them back?" asked the inspector.

"Call who back?" the man asked.

"The fish."

"What fish?" asked the man with a smile.

Two boys are fishing at a quiet lake off the beaten track. Suddenly, a fishing inspector jumps out of the bushes behind them.

Immediately, one of the boys throws down his rod and starts running away from the lake. The inspector chases him, until after about a mile he finally manages to grab the boy's shirt and pull him to a stop.

"Let's see your fishing license!" the inspector gasps.

The boy pulls out his wallet and shows the inspector a valid fishing license.

"Well," said the inspector, confused. "You must be a real moron! You don't have to run away from me if you have a valid license!"

"I know that," replies the boy. "But my friend back there, well, he doesn't have one."

A fishing riddle

ON a sunny morning, two fathers and two sons went fishing. Each one of them caught one fish. When they went home, there were only three fish. Why?

Answer: Because a grandfather, a father and a son went fishing.

JANE went to visit Margaret one Saturday afternoon. "Where's your husband, Harry?" asked Margaret.

"Out fishing again," answered Jane.

"Do you really believe him when he says he goes fishing every weekend?" said Margaret.

"Why shouldn't I?" Jane inquired.

"Well, maybe he's having an affair."

"No way," said Jane with a smile. "He comes home every time without any fish!"

FISHING season hadn't opened, but Jim was fishing in a nearby lake for trout.

A stranger wanders up to him and asks "Any luck?"

"Yeah," boasts Jim. "This is the greatest fishing spot. I caught ten here yesterday!"

"Really?" says the stranger. "By the way, do you know who I am?"

"Ah ... no," says Jim.

"Well, let me introduce myself," says the man, offering his hand. "I'm the new fishing inspector."

Jim turns red, then white, then sticks out his hand to shake the man's.

"Well," he says, 'I'm Jim. I'm the biggest liar in the country."

"WHAT's the biggest fish you ever caught?"

"The one that measured fourteen inches."

"That's not so big!"

"Between the eyes?"

You know you're a real fisherman when...

- Your local tackle shop has your credit card number on file.

- Your name is painted on a parking space at the launch ramp.

- You have a photo of the biggest fish you ever caught on your desk at work — but no photos of the kids.

- You think the word 'megabytes' means 'a wonderful day fishing'.

- Your kids know the weekend's started because the boat's gone.

"I caught a 20 pound king-fish last week."

"Were there any witnesses?"

"There sure were. If there weren't, I would have caught a 40 pound king-fish!"

NOTHING grows faster than a fish from the time it bites until the time it gets away!

RACHAEL's husband Peter died suddenly one day. Rachael phoned up the local paper to place an obituary.

"Hello, Fred. It's Rachael. I want to place Peter's obituary. How much does it cost?" she asked the editor.

The editor, Fred, replied, "Well, it'll cost one dollar per word."

"Alright," said Rachael. "I want the obituary to read:

PETER SMITH IS DEAD.

Fred had known Peter for years and was a little upset by such a short obituary.

"Look," he said. "I knew Peter well. I'll pay for half of the obituary out of my own pocket."

Rachael's face lit up and she replied "Great. I want it to read:

PETER SMITH IS DEAD,
FISHING GEAR FOR SALE.

AN OLD man on his death bed called in his family and said, "I must apologize to you all.

"I know I haven't been the perfect father and husband. I shamefully admit that I spent as much of my life as I could on the streams.

"I was rarely at home during the fishing seasons and I spent too much time at the fly shop, and too much money on rods and lines and reels."

He paused here to rest for a minute, and then continued. "I've been a terrible father and husband, and I hope you will forgive me."

Finally he closed his eyes, smiled, and said in a half whisper to himself, "And on the other hand ... I have caught a helluva lot of trout!"

MONSTERS
OF THE DEEP!

Tales of terrifying sea monsters are as old as ocean-going ships. And although most sightings can be dismissed as products of the over-stimulated imaginations of superstitious seamen, some continue to baffle scientists even today.

Among the oldest recorded monsters are the "kraken", described in Scandinavian stories almost a thousand years ago. They were said to inhabit the oceans near Norway and Iceland.

Resembling a giant squid or octopus, the tentacles were so large the suckers resembled a ring of islands.

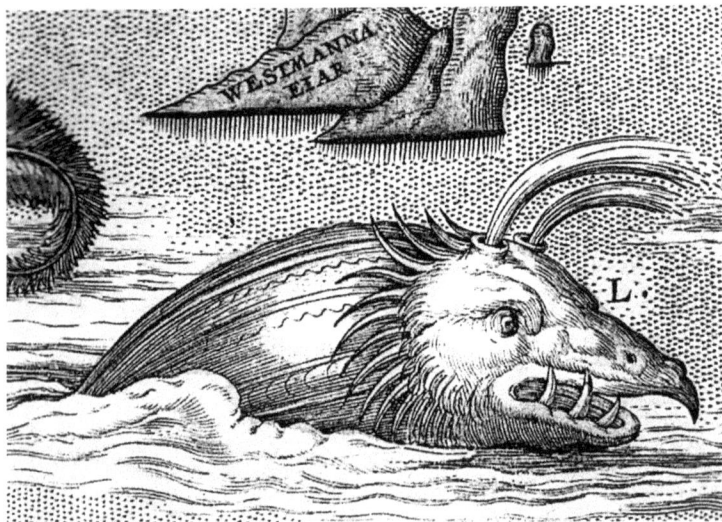

Seventeenth century mapmaker Abraham Ortelius filled in blank spaces with depictions of sea monsters, like this giant whale monster in the Atlantic Ocean off the coasts of Spain and Africa.

It was said the whirlpool the kraken (shown in an engraving above) created when diving could suck a vessel down to the depths, killing all on board.

So widespread was the belief in the existence of kraken that the British poet Alfred, Lord Tennyson wrote a poem to it halfway through the nineteenth century:

> *Below the thunders of the upper deep*
> *Far, far beneath in the abysmal sea*
> *His ancient, dreamless, uninvaded sleep*
> *The Kraken sleepeth...*
> *There hath he lain for ages and will lie...*
> *Until the latter fire shall heat the deep;*
> *Then once by man and angels to be seen,*
> *In roaring he shall rise and on the surface die.*

The stories of this terrifying sea monster received some authentication from bits of tentacles found in whale stomachs. Whales also showed terrible scars on their skins from battles with these fearsome creatures.

In 1853 a giant squid washed ashore in Denmark. Enterprising fishermen thought every dream had come true as they cut it up for bait.

Fortunately its enormous beak was preserved and in 1857 the monster received the scientific classification as belonging to the genus *Architeuthis*.

A giant kraken-like squid features prominently in Jules Verne's famous 1870 novel *20,000 Leagues Under the Sea*:

"It was a giant squid twenty-five feet long. It was heading toward the Nautilus, swimming backward very fast ...

"We could clearly make out the 250 suckers lining the inside of its tentacles, some of which fastened onto the glass panel of the lounge.

"The monster's mouth — a horny beak like that of a parakeet — opened and closed vertically.... What a whim of nature! A bird's beak in a mollusk!"

Giant squid usually dwell in deeper water by day, and come closer to the surface at night. Almost certainly sightings of these huge creatures inspired stories of the Kraken.

Even larger than the giant squid is the colossal

squid (*Mesonychoteuthis hamiltoni*). It outweighs all eight giant squid species.

The largest known colossal squid was captured in the freezing Ross Sea off New Zealand in February 2007. It weighed 1,091 pounds (495 kg) and was estimated to measure 33 feet (10 meters) in total length.

Fishermen on the vessel *San Aspiring* brought it to the surface as it fed on an Antarctic toothfish that had been caught off a long line. It would not let go of its prey so the fishermen enveloped it in a net, hauled it aboard, and froze it.

It was taken to the Museum of New Zealand Te Papa Tongarewa, where scientists thawed it in a bath of salt water.

Initially thought to be a male, closer inspection showed it to be a female whose ovaries contained thousands of eggs.

The beak is considerably smaller than some found in the stomachs of sperm whales, so scientists believe even larger squid live in the ocean depths.

The eye is 11 inches (27 cm) wide, making it the largest known animal eye.

Rivaling the colossal squid are the sea serpents — creatures with a snake-like body, spikes along the back and the head of a dragon.

Sound impossible? No, it's a giant oarfish, which

A team of US Navy seals hold a giant deep-ocean oarfish — a creature that probably inspired the belief in sea serpents.

can grow to over 50 feet (15 meters) long. It lives in the deep ocean and very rarely surfaces – but when it does it can easily be mistaken for a serpent.

Early sailors and cartographers certainly believed that sea serpents not only existed but were a threat to seafarers. Many claimed to have encountered them.

The oldest known depiction of a sea serpent is on a 1539 large wall map called the *Carta Marina*. This was the largest and most detailed map of Scandinavia at that time and show many sea monsters, including a blood-red sea serpent crushing a ship.

Olaus Magnus's *History of the Northern Peoples* (1555) has this to say about the map's giant sea serpent:

They who in Works of Navigation, on the Coasts of Norway, employ themselves in fishing or Merchandise, do all agree in this strange story, that there is a Serpent there which is of a vast magnitude, namely 200 foot long, and more — over 20 feet thick; and is

Crew try to hide as a sea serpent attacks a ship and devours a sailor, according to Olaus Magnus's *History of the Northern Peoples* (1555). The serpent was believed to live in a cave, shown in the picture where the tail is emerging. It could hunt on land and in the ocean.

wont to live in Rocks and Caves toward the Sea-coast about Berge: which will go alone from his holes in a clear night, in Summer, and devour Calves, Lambs, and Hogs, or else he goes into the Sea to feed on Polypus [octopus], Locusts [lobsters], and all sorts of Sea-Crabs. He hath commonly hair hanging from his neck a Cubit long, and sharp Scales, and is black, and he hath flaming shining eyes. This Snake disquiets the Shippers, and he puts up his head on high like a pillar, and catcheth away men, and he devours them ...

Much as we today may dismiss these creatures as superstitious nonsense, the ocean continues to hint at mysterious and frightening creatures that lurk in its depths.

An eye-witness sketch of a sea-serpent larger than a sailing ship as featured in Pontoppidan's *Natural History of Norway* (1753).

As recently as June 1914 it was reported that a huge 9 foot (2.7 meter) long great white shark was devoured by a much bigger creature.

Scientists had tagged the great white to track its movements. The tracking device disappeared — then washed up on a beach in Australia.

Amazingly, the instrument's readings showed a rapid rise in temperature from 46 degrees Fahrenheit (7.77 degrees Celsius) to 78F (25.55C) as it plunged 1902 feet (579 meters) towards the ocean bed.

Scientists believe the temperature soared when the great white and its tracking instrument were inside the digestive system of a much bigger creature that dived after snatching it.

What that creature is remains a mystery.

A FISHY TALE

by Jerome K. Jerome

Some people are under the impression that all that is required to make a good fisherman is the ability to tell lies easily and without blushing; but this is a mistake. Mere bald fabrication is useless; the veriest tyro can manage that.

It is in the circumstantial detail, the embellishing touches of probability, the general air of scrupulous – almost of pedantic – veracity, that the experienced angler is seen.

Anybody can come in and say, "Oh, I caught fifteen dozen perch yesterday evening;" or "Last Monday I landed a gudgeon, weighing eighteen pounds, and measuring three feet from the tip to the tail."

There is no art, no skill, required for that sort of thing. It shows pluck, but that is all.

No; your accomplished angler would scorn to tell a lie, that way. His method is a study in itself.

He comes in quietly with his hat on, appropriates the most comfortable chair, lights his pipe, and commences to puff in silence. He lets the youngsters brag away for a while, and then, during a momentary lull, he removes the pipe from his mouth, and remarks, as he knocks the ashes out against the bars:

"Well, I had a haul on Tuesday evening that it's not much good my telling anybody about."

"Oh! why's that?" they ask.

"Because I don't expect anybody would believe me if I did," replies the old fellow calmly, and without even a tinge of bitterness in his tone, as he refills his pipe, and requests the landlord to bring him three of Scotch, cold.

There is a pause after this, nobody feeling suf-

THE FISHING FANATIC'S Guide to Happiness 115

ficiently sure of himself to contradict the old gentleman. So he has to go on by himself without any encouragement.

"No," he continues thoughtfully; "I shouldn't believe it myself if anybody told it to me, but it's a fact, for all that. I had been sitting there all the afternoon and had caught literally nothing – except a few dozen dace and a score of jack; and I was just about giving it up as a bad job when I suddenly felt a rather smart pull at the line. I thought it was another little one, and I went to jerk it up.

"Hang me, if I could move the rod! It took me half-an-hour – half-an-hour, sir! – to land that fish; and every moment I thought the line was going to snap! I reached him at last, and what do you think it was?

"A sturgeon! a forty pound sturgeon! taken on a line, sir! Yes, you may well look surprised – I'll have another three of Scotch, landlord, please."

And then he goes on to tell of the astonishment of everybody who saw it; and what his wife said, when he got home, and of what Joe Buggles thought about it.

I asked the landlord of an inn up the river once, if it did not injure him, sometimes, listening to the tales that the fishermen about there told him; and he said:

"Oh, no; not now, sir. It did used to knock me over a bit at first, but, lor love you! me and the

Oceans and seas

Can you find the hidden words in this puzzle?
Level = Moderate. Words can go → ↓ ←

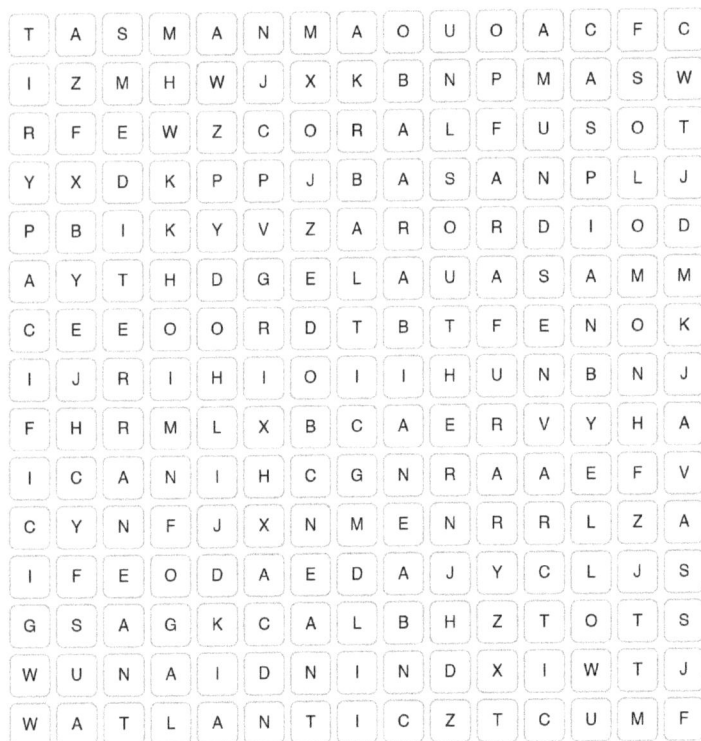

T	A	S	M	A	N	M	A	O	U	O	A	C	F	C
I	Z	M	H	W	J	X	K	B	N	P	M	A	S	W
R	F	E	W	Z	C	O	R	A	L	F	U	S	O	T
Y	X	D	K	P	P	J	B	A	S	A	N	P	L	J
P	B	I	K	Y	V	Z	A	R	O	R	D	I	O	D
A	Y	T	H	D	G	E	L	A	U	A	S	A	M	M
C	E	E	O	O	R	D	T	B	T	F	E	N	O	K
I	J	R	I	H	I	O	I	I	H	U	N	B	N	J
F	H	R	M	L	X	B	C	A	E	R	V	Y	H	A
I	C	A	N	I	H	C	G	N	R	A	A	E	F	V
C	Y	N	F	J	X	N	M	E	N	R	R	L	Z	A
I	F	E	O	D	A	E	D	A	J	Y	C	L	J	S
G	S	A	G	K	C	A	L	B	H	Z	T	O	T	S
W	U	N	A	I	D	N	I	N	D	X	I	W	T	J
W	A	T	L	A	N	T	I	C	Z	T	C	U	M	F

PACIFIC	SOUTHERN	SOLOMON
ATLANTIC	ARCTIC	TASMAN
MEDITERRANEAN	BALTIC	AMUNDSEN
INDIAN	CASPIAN	YELLOW
ARAFURA	CORAL	ARABIAN
DEAD	CHINA	
BLACK	JAVA	**Answer Page 160.**

missus we listens to `em all day now. It's what you're used to, you know. It's what you're used to."

I knew a young man once, he was a most con-
scientious fellow, and, when he took to fly-
fishing, he determined never to exaggerate his
hauls by more than twenty-five per cent.

"When I have caught forty fish," said he, "then I will tell people that I have caught fifty, and so on. But I will not lie any more than that, because it is sinful to lie."

But the twenty-five per cent plan did not work well at all. He never was able to use it. The greatest number of fish he ever caught in one day was three, and you can't add twenty-five per cent to three – at least, not in fish.

So he increased his percentage to thirty-three-and-a-third; but that, again, was awkward, when he had only caught one or two; so, to simplify matters, he made up his mind to just double the quantity.

He stuck to this arrangement for a couple of months, and then he grew dissatisfied with it. Nobody believed him when he told them that he only doubled, and he, therefore, gained no credit that way whatever, while his moderation put him at a disadvantage among the other anglers.

When he had really caught three small fish, and said he had caught six, it used to make him quite jealous to hear a man, whom he knew for a fact had only caught one, going about telling people he had landed two dozen.

So, eventually, he made one final arrangement with himself, which he has religiously held to ever since, and that was to count each fish that he caught as ten, and to assume ten to begin with.

For example, if he did not catch any fish at all, then he said he had caught ten fish – you could never catch less than ten fish by his system; that was the foundation of it. Then, if by any chance he really did catch one fish, he called it twenty, while two fish would count thirty, three forty, and so on.

It is a simple and easily worked plan, and there has been some talk lately of its being made use of by the angling fraternity in general.

Indeed, the Committee of the Thames Angler's Association did recommend its adoption about two years ago, but some of the older members opposed it. They said they would consider the idea if the number were doubled, and each fish counted as twenty.

If ever you have an evening to spare, up the river, I should advise you to drop into one of the little village inns, and take a seat in the tap-room. You will be nearly sure to meet one or two old rod-men, sipping their toddy there, and they will tell you enough fishy stories, in half an hour, to give you indigestion for a month.

George and I – I don't know what had become of Harris; he had gone out and had a shave, early in the afternoon, and had then come back and spent full forty minutes in pipe-claying his shoes, we had not seen him since – George and I, therefore, and the dog, left to ourselves, went for a walk to Wallingford on the second evening, and, coming home, we called in at a little riverside inn, for a rest, and other things.

We went into the parlor and sat down. There was an old fellow there, smoking a long clay pipe, and we naturally began chatting.

He told us that it had been a fine day today, and we told him that it had been a fine day yesterday, and then we all told each other that we thought it would be a fine day tomorrow; and George said the crops seemed to be coming up nicely.

After that it came out, somehow or other, that we were strangers in the neighborhood, and that we were going away the next morning.

Then a pause ensued in the conversation, during which our eyes wandered round the room. They finally rested upon a dusty old glass-case, fixed very high up above the chimney-piece, and containing a trout. It rather fascinated me, that trout; it was such a monstrous fish. In fact, at first glance, I thought it was a cod.

"Ah!" said the old gentleman, following the direction of my gaze, "fine fellow that, ain't he?"

Mystery maze #2

Start at top, end at bottom. Answer on Page 162.

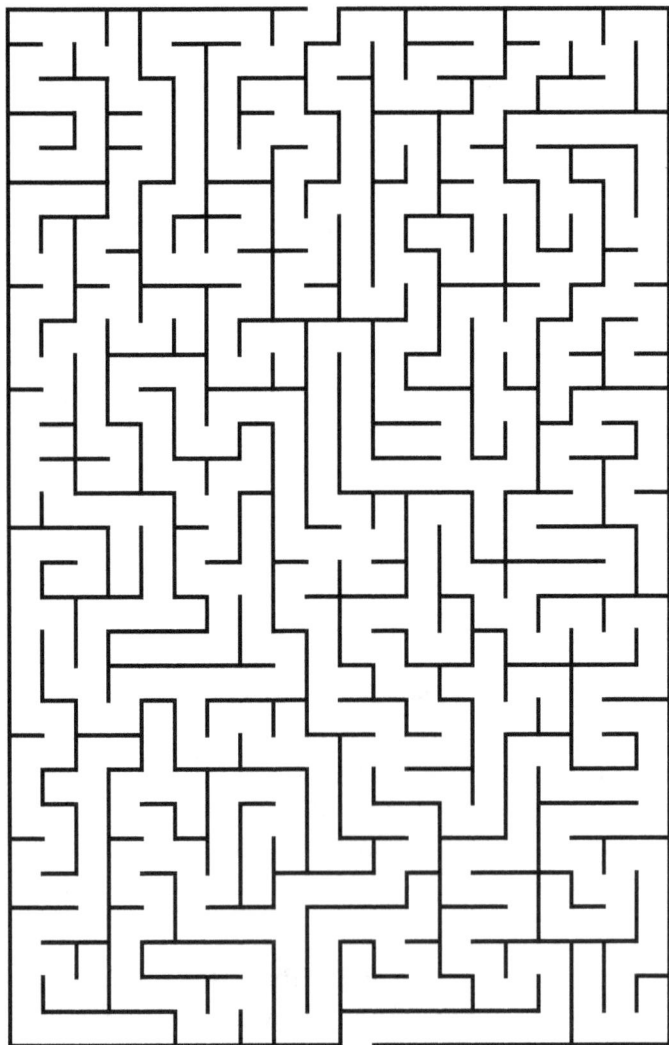

"Quite uncommon," I murmured; and George asked the old man how much he thought it weighed.

"Eighteen pounds six ounces," said our friend, rising and taking down his coat. "Yes," he continued, "it wur sixteen year ago, come the third o' next month, that I landed him. I caught him just below the bridge with a minnow. They told me he wur in the river, and I said I'd have him, and so I did. You don't see many fish that size about here now, I'm thinking. Good-night, gentlemen, good-night."

And out he went, and left us alone.

We could not take our eyes off the fish after that. It really was a remarkably fine fish. We were still looking at it, when the local carrier, who had just stopped at the inn, came to the door of the room with a pot of beer in his hand, and he also looked at the fish.

"Good-sized trout, that," said George, turning round to him.

"Ah! you may well say that, sir," replied the man; and then, after a pull at his beer, he added, "Maybe you wasn't here, sir, when that fish was caught?"

"No," we told him. We were strangers in the neighborhood.

"Ah!" said the carrier, "then, of course, how should you? It was nearly five years ago that I caught that trout."

"Oh! was it you who caught it, then?" said I.

"Yes, sir," replied the genial old fellow. "I caught him just below the lock — leastways, what was the lock then — one Friday afternoon; and the remarkable thing about it is that I caught him with a fly.

"I'd gone out pike fishing, bless you, never thinking of a trout, and when I saw that whopper on the end of my line, blest if it didn't quite take me aback. Well, you see, he weighed twenty-six pound. Goodnight, gentlemen, goodnight."

Five minutes afterwards, a third man came in, and described how he had caught it early one morning, with bleak; and then he left, and a stolid, solemn-looking, middle-aged individual came in, and sat down over by the window.

None of us spoke for a while; but, at length, George turned to the new comer, and said:

"I beg your pardon, I hope you will forgive the liberty that we — perfect strangers in the neighborhood — are taking, but my friend here and myself would be so much obliged if you would tell us how you caught that trout up there."

"Why, who told you I caught that trout!" was the surprised query.

We said that nobody had told us so, but somehow or other we felt instinctively that it was he who had done it.

"Well, it's a most remarkable thing — most remarkable," answered the stolid stranger, laughing; "because, as a matter of fact, you are quite right. I did catch it. But fancy your guessing it like that. Dear me, it's really a most remarkable thing."

And then he went on, and told us how it had taken him half an hour to land it, and how it had broken his rod. He said he had weighed it carefully when he reached home, and it had turned the scale at thirty-four pounds.

He went in his turn, and when he was gone, the landlord came in to us. We told him the various histories we had heard about his trout, and he was immensely amused, and we all laughed very heartily.

"Fancy Jim Bates and Joe Muggles and Mr. Jones and old Billy Maunders all telling you that they had caught it. Ha! ha! ha! Well, that is good," said the honest old fellow, laughing heartily. "Yes, they are the sort to give it ME, to put up in MY parlor, if THEY had caught it, they are! Ha! ha! ha!"

And then he told us the real history of the fish. It seemed that he had caught it himself, years ago, when he was quite a lad; not by any art or skill, but by that unaccountable luck that appears to always wait upon a boy when he plays the wag from school, and goes out fishing on a sunny afternoon, with a bit of string tied on to the end of a tree.

He said that bringing home that trout had saved him from a whacking, and that even his school-master had said it was worth the rule-of-three and practice put together.

He was called out of the room at this point, and George and I again turned our gaze upon the fish.

It really was a most astonishing trout. The more we looked at it, the more we marveled at it.

It excited George so much that he climbed up on the back of a chair to get a better view of it. And then the chair slipped, and George clutched wildly at the trout-case to save himself, and down it came with a crash, George and the chair on top of it.

"You haven't injured the fish, have you?" I cried in alarm, rushing up.

"I hope not," said George, rising cautiously and looking about.

But he had. That trout lay shattered into a thousand fragments – I say a thousand, but they may have only been nine hundred. I did not count them.

We thought it strange and unaccountable that a stuffed trout should break up into little pieces like that. And so it would have been strange and unaccountable, if it had been a stuffed trout, but it was not.

That trout was plaster-of-Paris.

(From *Three Men in a Boat*)

Fishinating Facts

Fish are amazing creatures — just ask any fishing fanatic. And no wonder. They have been around for more than 450 million years — more than double the time mammals have been on earth.

Today there are more species of fish than all the species of amphibians, reptiles, birds and mammals combined. And we still know absolutely nothing about at least a third of them. There are over 27,000 identified species of fish on the earth, with around 15,000 more fish species still to be identified.

Find that interesting? Below are some more fascinating facts about fish to keep you occupied while waiting for a catch.

Sharks

Can you stop a shark from attacking you by kissing it?

Fijians at one time certainly thought so. Father

Fishing vocabulary

Can you find the hidden words in this puzzle?
Level = Easy. Words can go →↓

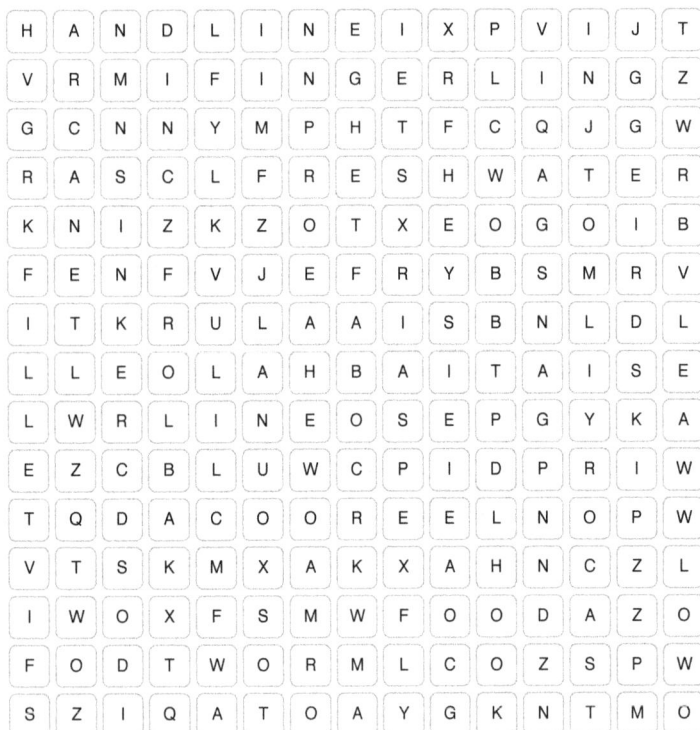

H	A	N	D	L	I	N	E	I	X	P	V	I	J	T
V	R	M	I	F	I	N	G	E	R	L	I	N	G	Z
G	C	N	N	Y	M	P	H	T	F	C	Q	J	G	W
R	A	S	C	L	F	R	E	S	H	W	A	T	E	R
K	N	I	Z	K	Z	O	T	X	E	O	G	O	I	B
F	E	N	F	V	J	E	F	R	Y	B	S	M	R	V
I	T	K	R	U	L	A	A	I	S	B	N	L	D	L
L	L	E	O	L	A	H	B	A	I	T	A	I	S	E
L	W	R	L	I	N	E	O	S	E	P	G	Y	K	A
E	Z	C	B	L	U	W	C	P	I	D	P	R	I	W
T	Q	D	A	C	O	O	R	E	E	L	N	O	P	W
V	T	S	K	M	X	A	K	X	A	H	N	C	Z	L
I	W	O	X	F	S	M	W	F	O	O	D	A	Z	O
F	O	D	T	W	O	R	M	L	C	O	Z	S	P	W
S	Z	I	Q	A	T	O	A	Y	G	K	N	T	M	O

HANDLINE	LINE	FLY
FINGERLING	REEL	HOOK
NYMPH	WORM	SNAG
FRESHWATER	FILLET	CAST
FRY	NET	SKIP
BAIT	SINKER	

Answer Page 159.

A.L. Laplante, a Catholic missionary, reported in 1930: "The natives drive the sharks into a large net, the shark kissers wade out, seize the man-eaters, kiss them on their up-turned bellies and fling them on their back.

"I don't know how they do it, but along the natives it is taken for granted that once a shark is kissed — upside down — that is the end of it."

After that, the Fijians believed, no shark in the area would attack local fishermen.

Nature's own shark repellent is found in the milky discharge of the Moses sole (Pardachirus mormoratus) that lives in the Red Sea.

According to Israeli scientists, the jaws of sharks coming into contact with this fluid are paralyzed.

What is the world's largest fish? The whale shark (*Rhincodon typus*), shown below, can weigh up to 15 tons and reach 49 feet (15 meters) in length.

It also produces the world's largest eggs — up to 13 inches (35cm) long.

Despite its fearsome size, the whale shark is completely harmless, feeding on plankton. To extract enough of the tiny creatures to feed itself, the whale shark filters over 400,000 gallons (1.5 million liters) of water every hour.

Hammerhead sharks have such sharp teeth that Maoris used them for shaving. Sharks replace teeth as they wear out, with tiger sharks replacing an astonishing 24,000 teeth between the ages of one and ten.

Sharks can detect blood even when it is diluted with sea water one part per million.

Sharks almost never suffer from cancer and also seem immune to many other diseases.

During the Second World War shark livers were used to extract huge amounts of vitamin A.

Angler fish

The Krøyer's deep sea angler fish, *Ceratias holboelli*, (opposite) is found at depths of 1000-2000m (3300-6600 ft). Because it is so dark down there, the angler fish lures prey with a bioluminescent lure that projects from its forehead.

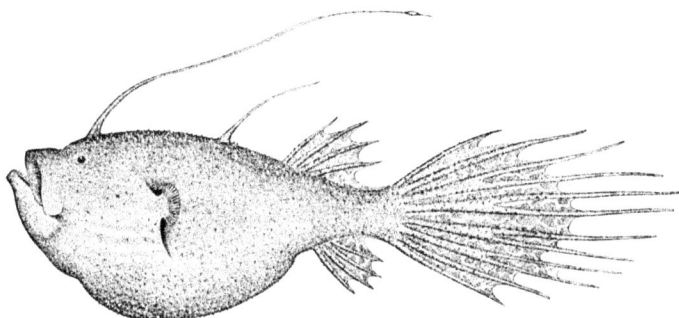

Even more amazing is the size difference between male and female angler fish. The latter can reach 47 inches (1.2 meters), while the male is a mere 2.2 inches (6 cm) long. The female can weigh 1000 times as much as the male.

The tiny male lives as a parasite on his partner. He makes small cuts in her skin with his sharp teeth, then "grows" into her body.

Eventually he loses his eyes, mouth and digestive tract, extracting nourishment directly from her bloodstream. Only his respiratory system continues to function, as do his sexual organs.

When ready to "mate" the female releases hormones in her blood that trigger the male to release sperm to fertilize her eggs.

The male can attach himself to any part of her body, even the head, and females have been found with several males clinging to them.

Octopus

The sex life of the octopus is quite bizarre. The male uses a special arm called a hectocotylus to massage the female's body. When both are sexually aroused their bodies suddenly change color and the mating process begins.

The male inserts the spoon-shaped tip of the reproductive arm into the female's mantle cavity. Packets of sperm flow along a groove on the underside of this arm and transfers to the female. Its job done, the male dies within months.

Sometimes the arm breaks off during mating, leaving a section dangling from the female. At one time these were considered parasitic worms. Eventually the male's broken arm regenerates.

The female of some species can keep the sperm alive until her eggs mature. She lays about 200,000 eggs — but only one or two reach maturity.

How do you kill an octopus without a weapon? If you're a fisherman on the Kiribati Islands, in the central Pacific, you bite them between the eyes!

Octopus meat is a delicacy to the islanders, who hunt the agile creatures in pairs.

When they spot a large one, a fisherman approaches it head-on to attract its attention, while the other one approaches from the side and bites the octopus between the eyes. This damages the brain and the creature is easy to catch.

The octopus is the most intelligent invertebrate and one of the cleverest creatures found in the ocean, with a mental capacity similar to that of a domestic cat.

They have been trained to remove the cork from a bottle and tests have shown they can remember things for considerable time.

They are also amazing escape artists. At a New York aquarium an octopus measuring 36 inches (90 cm) across managed to squeeze through a slit in box only one-eighth inch (3mm) wide.

Seahorse

The ancient philosopher Pliny prescribed the ashes of seahorses as a cure both for the bite of a rabid dog and for baldness.

Chinese eat dried seahorses as an aid to virility, while whole dried seahorses are worn as jewelry to enhance a lover's chances of winning the heart of a loved one. It is estimated that Chinese traditional medicine uses 150 million sea horses captured in the wild every year.

Sea horses are the slowest fishes in the ocean. The fastest are sailfish, swordfish, and marlin, reaching speeds of up to 70 mph (112 kph), which is faster than the speed limits on most highways!

Sea horses can "talk" to each other by making clicking sounds, according to researchers. Scientists have observed sea horses kept in separate tanks "calling" to one another at regular intervals. What information they are sharing is not known.

Seahorses not only have excellent eyesight, their eyes function independently on either side of the head. The result?

Big-belly seahorse

They can look to the front and to the back at the same time — great for spotting elusive prey! And they need it — baby seahorses can eat an amazing 3000 tiny crustacea a day.

Lifespans

Goldfish can live for decades. The oldest known goldfish, "Goldie," died in 2005 aged 45 years. The second oldest goldfish was "Tish" who died aged 43.

Some lobsters have longer life spans than both cats and dogs, living over 20 years.

Many rockfish beat that record hands down. Rougheye rockfish are can live over 200 years, longer than any other known species!

Size matters

The largest octopus is the Pacific Giant Octopus. The size of a pea when born, by two years old it can be 30 ft (9.1 m) across and weigh 150 pounds (68.2 kg).

The world's smallest catfish, the candiru found in Brazil, is also one of the most dangerous. About the size of a matchstick, it actively attacks humans in their most vulnerable parts.

Locals who go swimming in waters where candiru live protect their genitals with special palm leaf covers because the tiny fish can wriggle into the urethral openings of both males and females.

They have spines that point backwards, so the only way to remove them is through surgery. The pain they cause is said to be excruciating.

Birth fathers

Ever heard of a male giving birth? If not, you've not studied the reproductive habits of seahorses.

During a mating dance, the female squirts her eggs into the male's brood pouch. He fertilizes them in the pouch as she swims away, leaving him to incubate the eggs until they are ready to hatch. The males are very generous fathers — if the first female does not fill their pouch, they will accept eggs from other females as well.

Around 45 days later, the male starts to contract his pouch muscles, ejecting the near-transparent new-born seahorses in groups of two or three. This can take several days, as the males can incubate and "give birth" to as many as 14,000 offspring. The babies are almost exact clones of their parents — but at only a few millimeters in length, they are much, much smaller.

Some male catfish also incubate the eggs — not in a pouch but, even more bizarrely, in their mouth. The female transfers about 30 large eggs into her mate's mouth, which stretches enormously to accommodate them.

The male does not eat during the four weeks they take to hatch. When they do hatch they are about 2 inches (5cm) long, so the male's mouth has to stretch even wider until he can "give birth" by spitting them out. And while on the subject of mouths: catfish have over 27,000 taste buds, whereas humans have only 9,000.

A male Bangaii Cardinalfish incubates both eggs and babies in his mouth until the young are ready to swim on their own, a process known as "mouth brooding." Although it takes several weeks, the father will not eat until the eggs hatch.

THE GLADIATOR OF THE SEA

The thrilling tale of an epic battle by ZANE GREY

On the first morning of my fourth summer I was up at five. Fine, cool, fresh, soft dawn with a pale pink sunrise. Sea rippling with an easterly breeze. As the sun rose it grew bright and warm. We did not get started out on the water until eight o'clock. The east wind had whipped up a little chop that promised bad. But the wind gradually died down and the day became hot. Great thunderheads rose over the mainland, proclaiming heat on the desert. We saw scattered sheerwater ducks and a school of porpoises; also a number of splashes that I was sure were made by swordfish.

The first broadbill I sighted had a skinned tail, and evidently had been in a battle of some kind. We circled him three times with flying-fish bait and once with barracuda, and as he paid no attention to them we left him. This fish leaped half out on two occasions, once showing his beautiful proportions, his glistening silver white, and his dangerous-looking rapier.

The second one leaped twice before we neared him. And as we made a poor attempt at circling him, he saw the boat and would have none of our offers.

The third one was skimming along just under the surface, difficult to see. After one try at him we lost him.

They were not up on the surface that day, as they are when the best results are obtained. The east wind may have had something to do with that. These fish would average about three hundred pounds each. Captain Dan says the small ones are more wary, or not so hungry, for they do not strike readily.

I got sunburnt and a dizzy headache and almost

seasick. Yet the day was pleasant. The first few days are always hard, until I get broken in.

Next morning the water and conditions were ideal. The first two swordfish we saw did not stay on the surface long enough to be worked. The third one stayed up, but turned away from the bait every time we got it near him. So we left him.

About noon I sighted a big splash a mile off shoreward, and we headed that way. Soon I sighted fins. The first time round we got the bait right and I felt the old thrill. He went down. I waited; but in vain.

He leaped half out, and some one snapped a picture. It looked like a fortunate opportunity grasped. We tried him again, with flying-fish and barracuda. But he would not take either. Yet he loafed around on the surface, showing his colors, quite near the boat. He leaped clear out once, but I saw only the splash. Then he came out sideways, a skittering sort of plunge, lazy and heavy.

He was about a three-hundred pounder, white and blue and green, a rare specimen of fish. We tried him again and drew a bait right in front of him. No use! Then we charged him – ran him down. Even then he was not frightened, and came up astern. At last, discouraged at his indifference, we left him.

This day was ideal up to noon. Then the sun got

very hot. My wrists were burnt, and neck and face. My eyes got tired searching the sea for fins. It was a great game, this swordfishing, and beat any other I ever tried, for patience and endurance. The last fish showed his cunning. They were all different, and a study of each would be fascinating and instructive.

Next morning was fine. There were several hours when the sea was smooth and we could have sighted a swordfish a long distance. We went eastward of the ship course almost over to Newport. At noon a westerly wind sprang up and the water grew rough. It took some hours to be out of it to the leeward of the island.

I saw a whale bend his back and sound and lift his flukes high in the air – one of the wonder sights of the ocean.

It was foggy all morning, and rather too cool. No fish of any kind showed on the surface. One of those inexplicably blank days that are inevitable in sea angling.

When we got to the dock we made a discovery. There was a kink in my leader about one inch above the hook. Nothing but the sword of old *Xiphius gladius* could have made that kink! Then I remembered a strange, quick, hard jerk that had taken my bait, and which I thought had been done by a shark. It was a swordfish striking the bait off!

Next day we left the dock at six fifteen, Dan and I alone. The day was lowering and windy – looked bad. We got out ahead of every one. Trolled out five miles, then up to the west end. We got among the Japs fishing for albacore.

About eleven I sighted a big barracuda. We dragged a bait near him and he went down with a flirt of his tail. My heart stood still. Dan and I both made sure it was a strike. But, no! He came up far astern, and then went down for good.

The sea got rough. The wind was chilling to the bone. Sheerwater ducks were everywhere, in flocks and singly. Saw one yellow patch of small bait fish about an inch long. This patch was forty yards across. No fish appeared to be working on it.

Dan sighted a big swordfish. We made for him. Dan put on an albacore. But it came off before I could let out the line. Then we tried a barracuda. I got a long line out and the hook pulled loose. This was unfortunate and aggravating. We had one barracuda left. Dan hooked it on hard.

"That'll never come off!" he exclaimed. We circled old Xiphius, and when about fifty yards distant he lifted himself clear out – a most terrifying and magnificent fish. He would have weighed four hundred. His colors shone – blazed – purple blue, pale green, iridescent copper, and flaming silver.

Then he made a long, low lunge away from us. I bade him good-by, but let the barracuda drift back.

Types of boats

Can you find the hidden words in this puzzle?
Level = Easy. Words can go ➔ ⬇

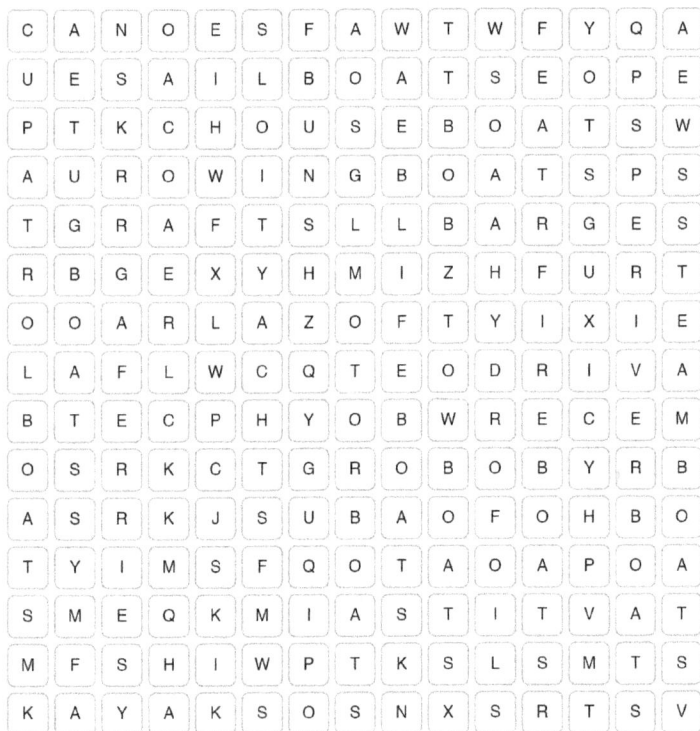

C	A	N	O	E	S	F	A	W	T	W	F	Y	Q	A
U	E	S	A	I	L	B	O	A	T	S	E	O	P	E
P	T	K	C	H	O	U	S	E	B	O	A	T	S	W
A	U	R	O	W	I	N	G	B	O	A	T	S	P	S
T	G	R	A	F	T	S	L	L	B	A	R	G	E	S
R	B	G	E	X	Y	H	M	I	Z	H	F	U	R	T
O	O	A	R	L	A	Z	O	F	T	Y	I	X	I	E
L	A	F	L	W	C	Q	T	E	O	D	R	I	V	A
B	T	E	C	P	H	Y	O	B	W	R	E	C	E	M
O	S	R	K	C	T	G	R	O	B	O	B	Y	R	B
A	S	R	K	J	S	U	B	A	O	F	O	H	B	O
T	Y	I	M	S	F	Q	O	T	A	O	A	P	O	A
S	M	E	Q	K	M	I	A	S	T	I	T	V	A	T
M	F	S	H	I	W	P	T	K	S	L	S	M	T	S
K	A	Y	A	K	S	O	S	N	X	S	R	T	S	V

BARGES — CANOES — FERRIES — FIREBOATS — HOUSEBOATS — HYDROFOILS — KAYAKS — LIFEBOATS — MOTORBOATS — PATROLBOATS — RAFTS — RIVERBOATS — ROWINGBOATS — SAILBOATS — STEAMBOATS — TOWBOATS — TUGBOATS — YACHTS

Answer Page 161.

We waited a long time while the line slowly bagged, drifting toward us. Suddenly I felt a quick, strong pull. It electrified me. I yelled to Dan. He said, excitedly, "Feed it to him!" but the line ceased to play out. I waited, slowly losing hope, with my pulses going back to normal.

After we drifted for five minutes I wound in the line. The barracuda was gone and the leader had been rolled up. This astounded us. That swordfish had taken my bait. I felt his first pull. Then he had come toward the boat, crushing the bait off the hook, without making even a twitch on the slack line.

It was heartbreaking. But we could not have done any different. Dan decided the fish had come after the teasers. This experience taught us exceeding respect for the broadbill.

Again we were off early in the morning. Wind outside and growing rough. Sun bright until off Isthmus, when we ran into fog. The Jap albacore-boats were farther west. Albacore not biting well. Sea grew rough. About eleven thirty the fog cleared and the sea became beautifully blue and white-crested.

I was up on the deck when a yell from below made me jump. I ran back. Some one was holding my rod, and on the instant that a huge swordfish got the bait had not the presence of mind to throw off the drag and let out line. We hurried to put on another flying-fish and I let out the line. Soon Dan yelled, "There he is – behind your bait!"

I saw him – huge, brown, wide, weaving after my bait. Then he hit it with his sword. I imagined I could feel him cut it. Winding in, I found the bait cut off neatly back of the head. While Dan hurried with another bait I watched for the swordfish, and saw him back in the wake, rather deep. He was following us. It was an intensely exciting moment. I let the bait drift back.

Almost at once I felt that peculiar rap at my bait, then another. Somehow I knew he had cut off another flying-fish. I reeled in. He had severed this bait in the middle. Frantically we baited again. I let out a long line, and we drifted. Hope was almost gone when there came a swift tug on my line, and then the reel whirred. I thumbed the pad lightly. Dan yelled for me to let him have it. I was all tingling with wonderful thrills. What a magnificent strike! He took line so fast it amazed me.

All at once, just as Dan yelled to hook him, the reel ceased to turn, the line slacked. I began to jerk hard and wind in, all breathless with excitement and frenzy of hope. Not for half a dozen pumps and windings did I feel him. Then heavy and strong came the weight.

I jerked and reeled. But I did not get a powerful strike on that fish. Suddenly the line slacked and my heart contracted. He had shaken the hook. I reeled in. Bait gone! He had doubled on me and run as swiftly toward the boat as he had at first run from it.

The hook had not caught well. Probably he had just held the bait between his jaws. The disappointment was exceedingly bitter and poignant. My respect for Xiphius increased in proportion to my sense of lost opportunity. This great fish thinks! That was my conviction.

We sighted another that refused to take a bait and soon went down.

We had learned the last few days that broadbills will strike when not on the surface, just as Marlin swordfish do.

On our next day out we had smooth sea all morning, with great, slow-running swells, long and high, with deep hollows between. Vast, heaving bosom of the deep! It was majestic. Along the horizon ran dark, low, lumpy waves, moving fast. A thick fog, like a pall, hung over the sea all morning.

About eleven o'clock I sighted fins. We made a circle round him, and drew the bait almost right across his bill. He went down. Again that familiar waiting, poignant suspense!… He refused to strike.

Next one was a big fellow with pale fins. We made a perfect circle, and he went down as if to take the bait!… But he came up. We tried again.

Same result. Then we put on an albacore and drew that, tail first, in front of him. Slowly he swam toward it, went down, and suddenly turned and shot away, leaving a big wake. He was badly scared by that albacore.

Next one we worked three times before he went down, and the last one gave us opportunity for only one circle before he sank.

They are shy, keen, and wise.

The morning following, as we headed out over a darkly rippling sea, some four miles off Long Point, where we had the thrilling strikes from the big swordfish, and which place we had fondly imagined was our happy hunting-ground – because it was near shore and off the usual fishing course out in the channel – we ran into Boschen fighting a fish.

This is a spectacle not given to many fishermen, and I saw my opportunity.

With my glass I watched Boschen fight the swordfish, and I concluded from the way he pulled that he was fast to the bottom of the ocean. We went on our way then, and that night when I got in I saw his wonderful swordfish, the world's record we all knew he would get some day. Four hundred and sixty-three pounds! And he had the luck to kill this great fish in short time.

My friend Doctor Riggin, a scientist, dissected this fish, and found that Boschen's hook had torn into the heart. This strange feature explained the easy capture, and, though it might detract some-what from Boschen's pride in the achievement, it certainly did not detract from the record.

That night, after coming in from the day's hunt for swordfish, Dan and I decided to get good bait. At five thirty we started for seal rocks.

The sun was setting, and the red fog over the west end of the island was weird and beautiful. Long, slow swells were running, and they boomed inshore on the rocks. Seals were barking – a hoarse, raucous croak. I saw a lonely heron silhouetted against the red glow of the western horizon.

We fished – trolling slowly a few hundred yards offshore – and soon were fighting barracuda, which we needed so badly for swordfish bait.

They strike easily, and put up a jerky kind of bat-tle. They are a long, slim fish, yellow and white in the water, a glistening pale bronze and silver when landed. I hooked a harder-fighting fish, which, when brought in, proved to be a white sea-bass, a very beautiful species with faint purplish color and mottled opal tints above the deep silver.

Next morning we left the bay at six thirty. It was the calmest day we had had in days. The sea was like a beveled mirror, oily, soft, and ethereal, with low swells barely moving. An hour and a half out we were alone on the sea, out of sight of land, with the sun faintly showing, and all around us, enclosing and mystical, a thin haze of fog.

Alone, alone, all alone on a wide, wide sea! This was wonderful, far beyond any pursuit of swordfish.

We sighted birds, gulls, and ducks floating like bits of colored cork, and pieces of kelp, and at length a broadbill. We circled him three times with barracuda, and again with a flying-fish. Apparently he had no interest in edibles. He scorned our lures. But we stayed with him until he sank for good.

Then we rode the sea for hours, searching for fins.

At ten forty we sighted another. Twice we drew a fresh fine barracuda in front of him, which he refused. It was so disappointing, in fact, really sickening.

Dan was disgusted. He said, "We can't get them to bite!"

And I said, "Let's try again!"

So we circled him once more. The sea was beautifully smooth, with the slow swells gently heaving. The swordfish rode them lazily and indifferently. His dorsal stood up straight and stiff, and the big sickle-shaped tail-fin wove to and fro behind. I gazed at them longingly, in despair, as unattainable. I knew of nothing in the fishing game as tantalizing and despairing as this sight.

We got rather near him this time, as he turned, facing us, and slowly swam in the direction of my bait. I could see the barracuda shining astern. Dan stopped the boat. I slowly let out line. The swordfish drifted back, and then sank.

I waited, intensely, but really without hope. And I watched my bait until it sank out of sight. Then followed what seemed a long wait. Probably it was really only a few moments. I had a sort of hopeless feeling. But I respected the fish all the more.

Then suddenly I felt a quiver of my line, as if an electric current had animated it. I was shocked keen and thrilling. My line whipped up and ran out.

"He's got it!" I called, tensely. That was a strong, stirring instant as with fascinated eyes I watched the line pass swiftly and steadily off the reel. I let him run a long way.

Then I sat down, jammed the rod in the socket, put on the drag, and began to strike. The second powerful sweep of the rod brought the line tight and I felt that heavy live weight. I struck at least a dozen times with all my might while the line was going off the reel.

The swordfish was moving ponderously. Presently he came up with a great splash, showing his huge fins, and then the dark, slender, sweeping sword. He waved that sword, striking fiercely at the leader. Then he went down. It was only at this moment I realized I had again hooked a broadbill.

Mystery maze #3

Start at top, end at bottom. Answer on Page 162.

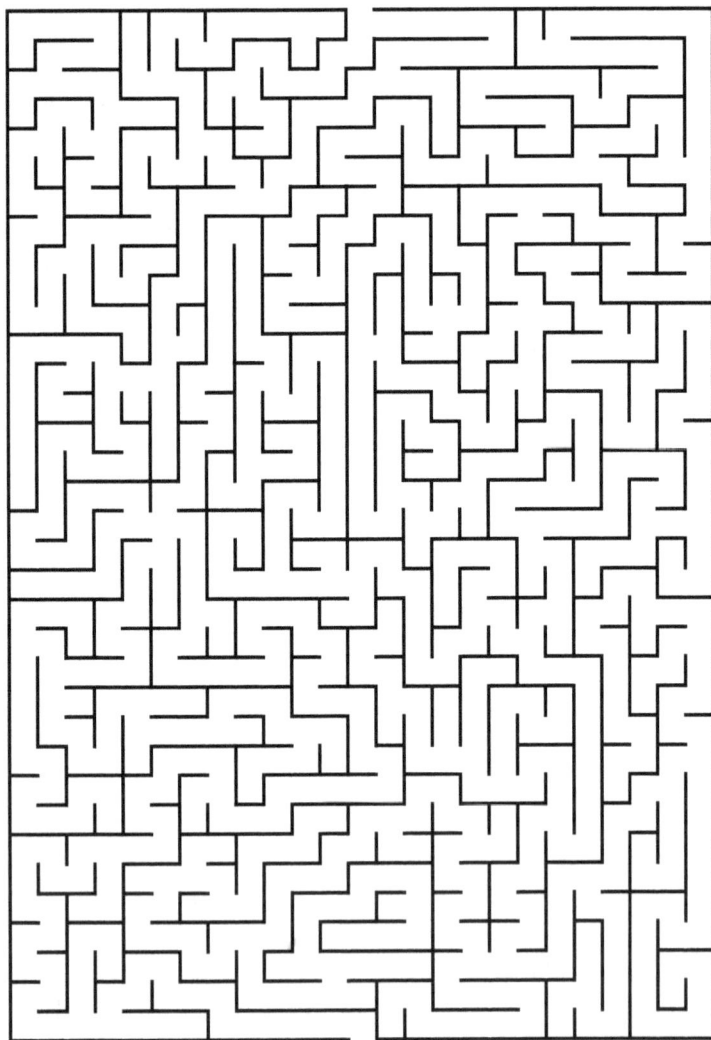

Time, ten forty-five.

The fight was on.

For a while he circled the boat and it was impossible to move him a foot. He was about two hundred and fifty yards from us. Every once in a while he would come up. His sword would appear first, a most extraordinary sight as it pierced the water. We could hear the swish. Once he leaped half out. We missed this picture. I kept a steady, hard strain on him, pumping now and then, getting a little line in, which he always got back.

The first hour passed swiftly with this surface fight alternating with his slow heavy work down. However, he did not sound.

About eleven forty-five he leaped clear out, and we snapped two pictures of him. It was a fierce effort to free the hook, a leap not beautiful and graceful, like that of the Marlin, but magnificent and dogged.

After this leap he changed his tactics. Repeatedly I was pulled forward and lifted from my seat by sudden violent jerks. They grew more frequent and harder. He came up and we saw how he did that. He was facing the boat and batting the leader with his sword.

This was the most remarkable action I ever observed in a fighting fish. That sword was a weapon.

I could hear it hit the leader. But he did most of this work under the surface.

Every time he hit the leader it seemed likely to crack my neck. The rod bent, then the line slackened so I could feel no weight, the rod flew straight. I had an instant of palpitating dread, feeling he had freed himself – then harder came the irresistible, heavy drag again.

This batting of the leader and consequent slacking of the line worried Dan, as it did me. Neither of us expected to hold the fish. As a performance it was wonderful. But to endure it was terrible. And he batted that leader at least three hundred times!

In fact, every moment or two he banged the leader several times for over an hour. It almost wore me out. If he had not changed those tactics again those jerks would have put a kink in my neck and back. But fortunately he came up on the surface to thresh about some more.

Again he leaped clear, affording us another chance for a picture. Following that he took his first long run. It was about one hundred yards and as fast as a Marlin. Then he sounded. He stayed down for half an hour. When he came up somewhat he seemed to be less resistant, and we dragged him at slow speed for several miles.

At the end of three hours I asked Dan for the harness, which he strapped to my shoulders. This afforded me relief for my arms and aching hands, but the straps cut into my back, and that hurt. The harness enabled me to lift and pull by a movement of shoulders. I worked steadily on him for an hour, five different times getting the two-hundred-foot mark on the line over my reel.

When I tired Dan would throw in the clutch and drag him some more. Once he followed us without strain for a while; again we dragged him two or three miles. And most remarkable of all, there was a period of a few moments when he towed us. A wonderful test for a twenty-four-strand line!

We made certain of this by throwing papers overboard and making allowance for the drift. At that time there was no wind. I had three and one-half hours of perfectly smooth water.

It was great to be out there on a lonely sea with that splendid fish. I was tiring, but did not fail to see the shimmering beauty of the sea, the playing of albacore near at hand, the flight of frightened flying-fish, the swooping down of gulls, the dim shapes of boats far off, and away above the cloud-bank of fog the mountains of California.

About two o'clock our indefatigable quarry began to belabor the leader again. He appeared even more vicious and stronger. That jerk, with its ragged, rough loosening of the line, making me feel the hook was tearing out, was the most trying action any fish ever worked on me. The physical effort necessary to hold him was enough, without that onslaught on my leader.

Again there came a roar of water, a splash, and his huge dark-blue and copper-colored body surged on the surface. He wagged his head and the long black sword made a half-circle. The line was taut from boat to fish in spite of all I could do in lowering my rod. I had to hold it up far enough to get the spring. There was absolutely no way to keep him from getting slack.

The dangerous time in fighting heavy, powerful fish is when they head toward the angler. Then the hook will pull out more easily than at any other time. He gave me a second long siege of these tactics until I was afraid I would give out. When he got through and sounded I had to have the back-rest replaced in the seat to rest my aching back.

Three o'clock came and passed. We dragged him awhile, and found him slower, steadier, easier to pull. That constant long strain must have been telling upon him. It was also telling upon me. As I tried to save some strength for the finish, I had not once tried my utmost at lifting him or pulling him near the boat.

Along about four o'clock he swung round to the west in the sun glare and there he hung, broadside, about a hundred yards out, for an hour. We had to go along with him.

The sea began to ripple with a breeze, and at length white-caps appeared. In half an hour it was rough, not bad, but still making my work exceedingly hard. I had to lift the rod up to keep the seat from turning and to hold my footing on the slippery floor. The water dripping from the reel had wet me and all around me.

At five o'clock I could not stand the harness any longer, so had Dan remove it. That was a relief. I began to pump my fish as in the earlier hours of the fight. Eventually I got him out of that broadside position away from us and to the boat. He took some line, which I got back. I now began to have confidence in being able to hold him. He had ceased batting the leader.

For a while he stayed astern, but gradually worked closer. This worried Dan. He was getting under the boat. Dan started faster ahead and still the swordfish kept just under us, perhaps fifty feet down. It was not long until Dan was running at full speed. But we could not lose the old gladiator! Then I bade Dan slow down, which he was reluctant to do. He feared the swordfish would ram us, and I had some qualms myself. At five thirty he dropped astern again and we breathed freer.

At this time I decided to see if I could pull him close. I began to pump and reel, and inch by inch, almost, I gained line. I could not tell just how far away he was, because the marks had worn off my line. It was amazing and thrilling, therefore, to

Fish body parts

Can you find the hidden words in this puzzle?
Level = moderate. Words can go →↓←

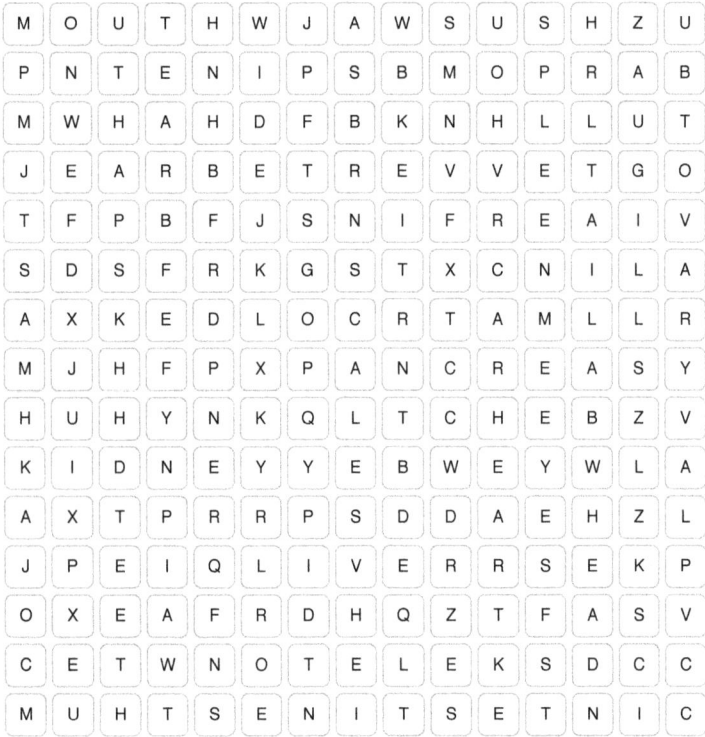

M	O	U	T	H	W	J	A	W	S	U	S	H	Z	U
P	N	T	E	N	I	P	S	B	M	O	P	R	A	B
M	W	H	A	H	D	F	B	K	N	H	L	L	U	T
J	E	A	R	B	E	T	R	E	V	V	E	T	G	O
T	F	P	B	F	J	S	N	I	F	R	E	A	I	V
S	D	S	F	R	K	G	S	T	X	C	N	I	L	A
A	X	K	E	D	L	O	C	R	T	A	M	L	L	R
M	J	H	F	P	X	P	A	N	C	R	E	A	S	Y
H	U	H	Y	N	K	Q	L	T	C	H	E	B	Z	V
K	I	D	N	E	Y	Y	E	B	W	E	Y	W	L	A
A	X	T	P	R	R	P	S	D	D	A	E	H	Z	L
J	P	E	I	Q	L	I	V	E	R	R	S	E	K	P
O	X	E	A	F	R	D	H	Q	Z	T	F	A	S	V
C	E	T	W	N	O	T	E	L	E	K	S	D	C	C
M	U	H	T	S	E	N	I	T	S	E	T	N	I	C

FINS	GILLS	HEART
EYES	JAWS	SPLEEN
SCALES	SKELETON	PANCREAS
TAIL	VERTEBRAE	OVARY
HEAD	INTESTINES	SPINE
MOUTH	LIVER	
TEETH	KIDNEY	Answer Page 160.

suddenly see the end of the double line appear.

Dan yelled. So did I. Like a Trojan I worked till I got that double line over my reel. Then we all saw the fish. He was on his side, swimming with us – a huge, bird-shaped creature with a frightful bill. Dan called me to get the leader out of water and then hold. This took about all I had left of strength. The fish wavered from side to side, and Dan feared he would go under the boat. He ordered me to hold tight, and he put on more speed.

This grew to be more than I could stand. It was desperately hard to keep the line from slipping. And I knew a little more of that would lose my fish.

So I called Dan to take the leader. With his huge gaff in right hand, Dan reached for the leader with his left, grasped it, surged the fish up and made a lunge. There came a roar and a beating against the boat. Dan yelled for another gaff. It was handed to him and he plunged that into the fish.

Then I let down my rod and dove for the short rope to lasso the sweeping tail. Fortunately he kept quiet a moment in which I got the loop fast.

It was then *Xiphius gladius* really woke up.

He began a tremendous beating with his tail. Both gaff ropes began to loosen, and the rope on his tail flew out of my hands. Dan got it in time. But it was slipping. He yelled for me to make a hitch somewhere. I was pulled flat in the cockpit, but scrambled up, out on the stern, and held on to that rope grimly while I tried to fasten it. Just almost impossible!

The water was deluging us. The swordfish banged the boat with sodden, heavy blows. But I got the rope fast. Then I went to Dan's assistance. The two of us pulled that tremendous tail up out of the water and made fast the rope. Then we knew we had him.

But he surged and strained and lashed for a long while. And side blows of his sword scarred the boat. At last he sagged down quiet, and we headed for Avalon. Once more in smooth water, we loaded him astern. I found the hook just in the corner of his mouth, which fact accounted for the long battle.

Doctor Riggin, the University of Pennsylvania anatomist, and classmate of mine, dissected this fish for me. Two of the most remarkable features about *Xiphius gladius* were his heart and eye.

The heart was situated deep in just back of the gills. It was a big organ, exceedingly heavy, and the most muscular tissue I ever saw. In fact, so powerfully muscular was it that when cut the tissue contracted and could not be placed together again. The valves were likewise remarkably well developed and strong. This wonderful heart accounted for the wonderful vitality of the swordfish.

The eyes of a swordfish likewise proved the

wonder of nature. They were huge and prominent, a deep sea-blue set in pale crystal rims and black circles. A swordfish could revolve his eyes and turn them in their sockets so that they were absolutely protected in battle with his mates and rivals. The eye had a covering of bone, cup-shaped, and it was this bone that afforded protection. It was evident that when the eye was completely turned in the swordfish could not see at all. Probably this was for close battle.

The muscles were very heavy and strong, one attached at the rim of the eye and the other farther back. The optic nerve was as large as the median nerve of a man's arm – that is to say, half the size of a lead-pencil.

There were three coverings over the fluid that held the pupil. And these were as thick and tough as isinglass. Most remarkable of all was the ciliary muscle which held the capacity of contracting the lens for distant vision.

A swordfish could see as far as the rays of light penetrated in whatever depth he swam. I have always suspected he had extraordinary eyesight, and this dissection of the eye proved it. No fear a swordfish will not see a bait! He can see the boat and the bait a long distance.

Doctor Riggin found no sperm in any of the male fish he dissected, which was proof that swordfish spawn before coming to Catalina waters. They are a warm-water fish, and probably head off the Japan current into some warm, intersecting branch that leads to spawning-banks.

This was happy knowledge for me, because it will be good to know that when old *Xiphius gladius* is driven from Catalina waters he will be roaming some other place of the Seven Seas, his great sickle fins shining dark against the blue.

"WEEKEND FISHERMAN! — JUST LOOK AT THE POOR QUALITY OF THAT BAIT".

Fishing vocabulary answer

```
H  A  N  D  L  I  N  E
            F  I  N  G  E  R  L  I  N  G
      N  Y  M  P  H
      S        F  R  E  S  H  W  A  T  E  R
   N  I
F  E  N           F  R  Y     S
I  T  K                       N
L  E           B  A  I  T  A        S
L  R  L  I  N  E              G     K
E                                  I
T                 R  E  E  L        P
                           H     C
                     F     O     A
         W  O  R  M  L     O     S
                     Y     K     T
```

Watery words answer

```
R  I  V  E  R                    S  E  A
W  E  T                          S
R  W  A  V  E     P  O  N  D      P
I  O                    S        L
V  C                 T           A
U  E                 A           S
L  A                 G  B     H
E  N        S     S  N  R
T           T     W  A  E  F
T  C        R  E  N  A  O        R
I  A        E  L  T  K  A        A
D  L        A  L     E  M        P
E  M        M              R     I
            T  U  R  B  U  L  E  N  T  D
      W  A  T  E  R  F  A  L  L        S
```

Fish body parts answer

```
M  O  U  T  H  .  J  A  W  S  .  S  .  .  .
.  .  .  E  N  I  P  S  .  .  .  P  .  .  .
.  .  .  .  .  .  .  .  .  L  .  .  .
.  E  A  R  B  E  T  R  E  V  .  E  T  G  O
.  .  .  .  .  .  S  N  I  F  .  E  A  I  V
.  .  .  .  .  .  .  S  .  .  .  N  I  L  A
.  .  .  .  .  .  .  C  .  .  .  L  L  R
.  .  .  .  .  .  P  A  N  C  R  E  A  S  Y
.  .  .  .  .  .  .  L  .  H  E  .  .  .
K  I  D  N  E  Y  .  E  .  .  E  Y  .  .  .
.  .  T  .  .  .  S  .  .  A  E  H  .
.  .  E  .  L  I  V  E  R  R  S  E  .
.  .  E  .  .  .  .  .  .  T  .  A  .  .
.  .  T  .  N  O  T  E  L  E  K  S  D  .  .
.  .  H  .  S  E  N  I  T  S  E  T  N  I  .
```

Oceans and seas answer

```
T  A  S  M  A  N  .  .  .  .  .  A  C  .  .
.  .  M  .  .  .  .  .  .  .  M  A  S  .
.  .  E  .  .  C  O  R  A  L  .  U  S  O  .
.  .  D  .  .  .  .  B  A  S  A  N  P  L  .
P  .  I  .  .  .  .  A  R  O  R  D  I  O  .
A  .  T  .  .  .  .  L  A  U  A  S  A  M  .
C  .  E  .  .  .  .  T  B  T  F  E  N  O  .
I  .  R  .  .  .  .  I  I  H  U  N  .  N  J
F  .  R  .  .  .  .  C  A  E  R  .  Y  .  A
I  .  A  N  I  H  C  .  N  R  A  A  E  .  V
C  .  N  .  .  .  .  .  N  .  R  L  .  A
.  .  E  .  D  A  E  D  .  .  .  C  L  .  .
.  .  A  .  K  C  A  L  B  .  .  T  O  .  .
.  .  N  A  I  D  N  I  .  .  .  I  W  .  .
.  A  T  L  A  N  T  I  C  .  .  C  .  .  .
```

Types of boats answer

```
C   A   N   O   E   S
        S   A   I   L   B   O   A   T   S
P   T           H   O   U   S   E   B   O   A   T   S
A   U   R   O   W   I   N   G   B   O   A   T   S
T   G   R   A   F   T   S       L   B   A   R   G   E   S
R   B               Y       M   I       H   F       R   T
O   O               A       O   F   T   Y   I       I   E
L   A   F           C       T   E   O   D   R       V   A
B   T   E           H       O   B   W   R   E       E   M
O   S   R           T       R   O   B   O   B       R   B
A       R           S       B   A   O   F   O       B   O
T       I                   O   T   A   O   A       O   A
S       E                   A   S   T   I   T       A   T
        S                   T       S   L   S       T   S
K   A   Y   A   K   S       S       S               S
```

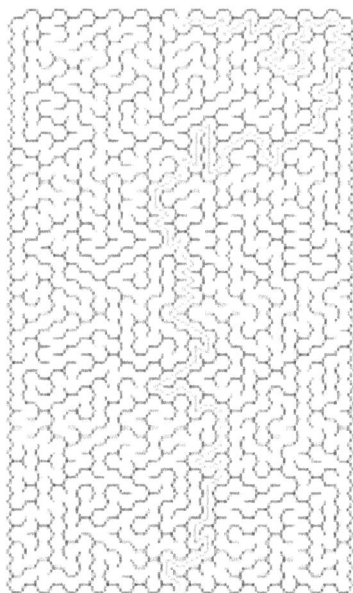

Mystery maze #1 answer

Mystery
maze
#2
answer

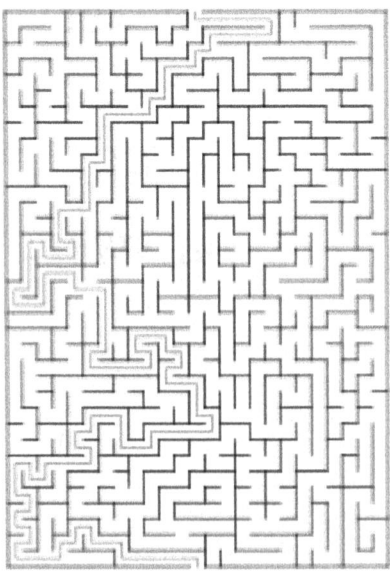

Mystery
maze
#3
answer

www.ingramcontent.com/pod-product-compliance
Lightning Source LLC
Chambersburg PA
CBHW060928040426
42445CB00011B/847